THE
DICK
SMITH
WAY

This book is dedicated to:
My wife, Louise, and children, Andrew, Justin and Monique, who give my life fulfilment; and to my parents, Ed and Joan, who gave me dreams, and unselfishly encouraged me to pursue them.

My Company

By Dick Smith

The love of quiet board rooms
Of softly shaded panes
Of ordered chairs and tables
Is running in your veins
Strong love of expensive paintings
Of security and well stocked bars
I know, but cannot share it
My love is otherwise.

I love a bright and noisy firm
A place of sweeping aims
Of quick dynamic decisions
Hard work and soaring gains
I love to joke and laugh
I love to talk and see
The challenge and excitement
The bright fun firm for me.

(with apologies to Dorothea Mackellar)

THE
DICK
SMITH
WAY

IKE BAIN

Sydney New York St.Louis San Francisco Auckland
Bogotá Caracas Lisbon London Madrid MexicoCity Milan
Montreal New Delhi SanJuan Singapore Tokyo Toronto

McGraw·Hill Australia

A Division of The **McGraw·Hill** Companies

Reprinted 2003 (twice)
Text © 2002 Ike Bain
Design © 2002 McGraw-Hill Australia Pty Ltd
Additional owners of copyright are acknowledged on the credits page.

National Library of Australia Cataloguing-in-Publication data:

Bain, Ike.
The Dick Smith way.

Includes index.
ISBN 0 074 71160 1.

1. Smith, Dick, 1944- . 2. Dick Smith Electronics. 3. Australian Geographic Pty. Ltd.
4. Entrepreneurship – Australia – Case studies. 5. Success in business – Australia –
Case studies. I. Title.

338.040994

Published in Australia by
McGraw-Hill Australia Pty Ltd
Level 2, 82 Waterloo Road, North Ryde NSW 2113, Australia

Acquisitions Editor: Javier Dopico
Editorial Consultant: Stuart Inder
Production Editor: Rosemary McDonald
Editor: Christine Eslick
Proofreader: Tim Learner
Indexer: Diane Harriman

Designer: Peter Evans
Cartoonist: Loui Silvestro
Cover photo: Pip Smith
Typeset in 12/15 pt Bembo by Peter Evans
Printed on 79 gsm bulky paperback by
McPherson's Printing Australia

Foreword

When people ask me the secret of success, my first response is 'Surround yourself with capable people'. For me, the best example of this is the partnership I developed with Ike Bain.

In 1972 Dick Smith Electronics had two small shops in Sydney's northern suburbs, one for repairing taxi radios and the other for selling electronic components. When I first met Ike I was working behind the counter of the retail shop to keep my costs down in an effort to trade out of receivership. But as you will read in the pages ahead, the road to success has many turns, and a few potholes. The shop was in a little old house, and when Ike came through the front door he asked incredulously, 'Is this Dick Smith Electronics?' He was expecting something different.

Just what he expected, Ike explains in his opening chapter, and we both had a laugh at the time. I quickly recognised that this tall, young Canadian was a genuine fellow radio enthusiast and that we shared a similar sense of humour. Even though Ike was only 20 years old, he seemed very self-assured. (I, by then, had reached the grand old age of 28!)

I offered him a job on the spot. He declined, as he said he was interested in joining the New South Wales Police Force, but we agreed to stay in touch. As he was leaving, I gave him a free street directory, and he seemed astounded by my generosity. (I happily leave you to read the rest of that story in the book, together with all the other good stories of our long and harmonious working partnership.) Fortunately for me, Ike didn't pursue his interest in the police, and within the year I had hired him as a radio technician.

Before long I made him a manager, and we quickly learned that we had a rare combination of very different, but complementary, personalities. I was the front man, and Ike brought administrative strength. I was good at generating ideas; Ike made sure they were communicated across the company and adhered to. I came up with outrageous ways to promote the business, and Ike was my sensible sounding board.

Ike was tough as a manager, but fair, so I made him my general manager, and he had the most incredible influence on the success of Dick Smith Electronics. After I sold that thriving business to Woolworths (simply because I decided I wanted a change of direction), I started the Australian Geographic company in 1985. Within two years Ike agreed to rejoin me as its chief executive officer—a role that I knew he would relish because it combined two of his passions, retailing and the great outdoors. I did not want to greatly expand Australian Geographic, but Ike had different ideas, as he relates here. The huge success of the retail arm of Australian Geographic was entirely due to Ike's abilities.

It's been fascinating reading Ike's reminiscences. Although I'd forgotten many of the stories he tells, I will always remember the lessons we learned from our mistakes. They are also recounted here, so others can learn too. I'm proud that we ran good honest businesses, paid our taxes, never went broke and gave work to many thousands of Australians.

Finally, one of my favourite incidents is the one Ike relates of the time the American electronics giant Tandy came to Sydney with the resources to crush fledgling businesses like Dick Smith Electronics, and how we organised a demonstration in front of their store. It was a lot of fun, and we received great press. You can imagine Ike's and my pleasure when in 2001 we read that Woolworths had taken a controlling interest in Tandy Australia, for it was just great to see an Aussie business taking over a foreign business for a change! Perhaps your business can do the same.

But one thing I am sure of. If you follow the advice that Ike presents so clearly and readably in these pages, you will be rewarded with success.

Dick Smith

Contents

Preface

About eighteen months ago I came across a forgotten file about a talk I gave in 1996 at the *Retailers Digest* Conference at the Sydney Convention Centre. The talk was entitled 'What has made us successful?' It was later published in the *National Business Bulletin*, and excerpts also appeared in *Inside Retailing*. In the file, my secretary had placed letters from people appreciative of what they had gleaned from reading about our experiences. As I read their comments I thought about how much more I could have told them if I had not been constrained by time at the conference. I began recording further points in my diary and on the computer. The result is this collection of business tips, insights into a business philosophy and, especially, practical lessons I learned from many years working with Dick Smith in two ventures he established at different times: Dick Smith Electronics and Australian Geographic Pty Ltd.

Dick used to say that he was just a simple bushwalker and transistor salesman. Well, I was just a simple country boy with a love of electronics, but I first learned from him how to put this interest to use in a business—Dick Smith Electronics—and then, day by day, week by week, how to run the business and, finally, to expand it. It was this early bond and our mutual desire to do well that resulted in us, over the years, combining our skills so successfully. This book enables me to thank Dick publicly for taking the risk and giving me, then a mere 20-year-old, the opportunity to join him on his incredible business journey. The unexpected manner of my joining him proves yet again that opportunities don't always show themselves in apparent or predictable ways.

Neither of us had any formative business training, and because we were also young and inexperienced, we had to learn the hard way through trial and error. We made a lot of errors, but we tried to learn from them. We were, as a result, very open to discovering how and why others were successful. Dick spent a lot of time asking people how they did things, and today he is still a great asker of questions. When we saw a good idea we tried it in the business, and if it worked we used it. When one of our people came up with a workable idea, we used it. We were always experimenting with ways of refining our emerging business formula, and if we discovered something that worked exceptionally well we didn't tamper with it. Those are still worthwhile lessons, and you'll find them in these pages, together with other practical, commonsense tips that we put to use—and together with others that didn't work, for there are lessons to be learned from those too!

I've written this book for business people (active or not), for those who hope to be in business one day and for people who might not have the slightest interest in a business career but would like to know why Dick Smith is so good at it. I hope you will be entertained by the sense of fun, enthusiasm and adventure that spills out of the Dick

Smith story, for fun, enthusiasm and adventure are Dick's natural approach to life. (And there's a lesson in that too!)

Of course, all businesses have help from many directions, and I thank all those people who have, over the years, been so generous in providing their time and motivation to me personally. Some I have been able to name in passing, but I have been very fortunate to have met so many other special people who gave me much more of themselves than they were required to. In business, you're only as good as the people you surround yourself with (which is yet another of Dick's sayings), and all of us who worked to build Dick Smith Electronics and Australian Geographic into two very successful companies know we were part of the best business school imaginable. Welcome to the class!

Acknowledgments

Special thanks to:

My wife Louise, for all her wonderful support, patience and understanding, not just during the writing of the book but during all the years of the business career behind the book; Joel Wacknov, for his encouragement and suggestions; Cres James, for his feedback; Javier Dopico of McGraw-Hill, who from the very beginning was enthused and so enjoyable and professional to work with; Dick and Pip Smith, two very special people I am lucky to have worked with, for their support; Bill James, author of *Top Deck Daze*, who inspired me; my hardworking editor, Stuart Inder, MBE, who kept me on track and did a brilliant job (Stuart and I began talking about this book over ten years ago and because of his enthusiasm and encouragement it came to fruition); Stephen Downes for some good recollections; Luke Fryer; Ross Jackson, who took time during his holidays to give me feedback; Geoff Newlyn, for anecdotal info; Terry Hunt, Steve Hawkins, Richard Wood, Valerie Reed, Will Pringle, Moyna Smeaton, Jan Dalton, for all their assistance; Bob Sessions, for his publishing advice; Jenny Mawter, for her encouragement; my son, Andrew, for his fantastic computer skills; and to all the wonderful people who shared the experiences in the book with me, a special thanks for the fond memories.

Part 1

WORKING WITH DICK SMITH

Chapter 1

Meeting Dick Smith, the car-radio nut

I met Dick Smith for the first time in 1972, when I was twenty. I'd seen his ad for radio transceivers in an electronics magazine, and as a young ham-radio enthusiast I hoped to buy from him my first *real* transmitter—one that I could speak into—to replace my existing low-powered transmitter that sent out only in Morse code. I was a newcomer to Sydney and had very little money, but I was excited by his ad and set off on my motorcycle to inspect the huge range it said he held at his shop in Atchison Street, in suburban St Leonards.

I rode up and down Atchison Street several times but I couldn't find the shop. On my last attempt a sign, 'Dick Smith Wholesale', finally caught my eye, but the sign wasn't on a huge shop as I had somehow expected, or even on a small one—it was on a little bungalow. I wandered up its garden path and into what would normally have been the lounge room, where this fellow with dark-rimmed glasses, and only a few years older than me, stood behind a small glass showcase.

He greeted me enthusiastically, but the shop was very Spartan and I was the only customer. I thought, 'This place

I first meet Dick Smith, this fellow with dark-rimmed glasses, and only a few years older than me, standing behind a small glass showcase.

has to be going broke!' In fact, Dick Smith Wholesale was in receivership, and the reason Dick was there serving customers was that he had decided he would get behind the counter himself and trade his way out. I asked to see his range of transceivers, and he looked a little sheepish as he pulled a small 1 watt 27 MHz handheld walkie-talkie off the shelf. It soon became obvious that this *was* his range!

He seemed a friendly and likeable person, and when I told him what I was looking for he offered to call a friend of his who had his transceiver up for sale, and he gave me the address. He then asked me what work I was in, and about my interests, and said, 'Why don't you come and work for me, servicing two-way radios?' I told him I would need to think about that.

As I was leaving he asked if I knew how to get to his friend's place. Without hesitating he brought out a pristine street directory and began to mark it up with a pen. I thought, 'Now why is he doing this to his new directory?' When he finished, he handed the directory to me, saying, 'Here, take this, it's yours. And tell your friends about us.'

I was amazed. I had walked into this fellow's unimpressive little shop, he could sell me nothing that I wanted, yet now he behaved as if he were enlisting a customer for life. I began to think that maybe I *should* work for him!

There is a postscript to this story. Late one evening many years later I was standing outside the Dick Smith Electronics headquarters shop after Dick and I had been working back in the office. The business was booming and I was in a reflective mood. I reminded Dick about the first time we met and said how much his spontaneous presentation of that street directory had meant to me. He burst out laughing. 'That street directory? We had thousands of those! They were out of date and we were giving one to everybody!'

I should have known, for by that time I knew a lot more about Dick's abilities as a salesman, and my respect for the way he does things—for the Dick Smith Way—has never dimmed. But with that street directory he taught me my first lesson. The lesson is: make your customers feel special and they will come back.

Ike Bain, electronics nut from Canada

I was born in Toronto, Canada in 1952. My father, Edgar, was in retail and my mother, Joan, was a schoolteacher. My father had temporarily escaped the small country town of Yarmouth, Nova Scotia, where five generations of the Bains, descendants of Scottish migrants, had sailed from the once famous seaport to foreign lands or worked the land on the small farm that has been held in the family since 1830.

I grew up on a dairy farm at Chegoggin, outside Yarmouth, on a bluff overlooking the Bay of Fundy. The farm was in poor condition, the timber buildings being over 120 years old, but my father worked hard, night after night sitting by the stove with pen and paper, doing long sums as he attempted to make things work financially. I would find these small pieces of paper scattered throughout the sheds, for whenever an idea came to him or an unexpected expense arose he would calculate the cash flow needed to make it viable. Watching him, I later realised, gave me an early appreciation of the importance of money.

At Chegoggin I also developed a love and respect for nature, something that was later to benefit me in my role at Australian Geographic. From the hill where the rambling farmhouse lay there was a 360 degree vista. We could see the Atlantic Ocean to the south and hear the pounding surf during the regular storms. From a nearby fishing village, small Grand Banks–style fishing boats worked, catching the prized Nova Scotian lobster and seining for herring and cod that were smoked in the smokehouses. To the north I could see my grandparents' farm, where generations of earlier Bains had lived out their lives. Summers seemed fleetingly short; we worked hard to make money from the cash crops we grew to supplement the dairy and I would go around the neighbours on my pushbike peddling—for 5 cents each—the cabbages from a couple of crop rows my father had said could be mine. It was another effective way for me to learn about business, although I didn't know I was learning.

When I was fourteen my brother got a crystal radio set for Christmas from Canada's famous Eaton catalogue. I loved that Eaton catalogue: it brought a whole department store into your home. I would read the copy over and over, and dream that one day I might be able to buy some of the products. The crystal set fascinated me because it operated on the minute current generated by the antenna and a buried earth point to produce a radio signal in your headphones. I would learn many years later that Dick's interest in electronics had been sparked by a crystal set too. I started to experiment with long, wire antennas strung between spruce trees and a timber pole mast I had cut and shaped, listening with the headphones intently for hours until one evening I detected a voice. To my joy I had picked up Armed Forces Radio & Television Service broadcasting from Greenville, North Carolina.

I now wanted a real shortwave radio. I placed a small ad in the classifieds of our local paper: 'Wanted, Old Radios'. To my surprise, people phoned me. I would pedal around on my pushbike and have a look. Most of the radios were what I'd advertised for—old and not in working order—

but it didn't matter, I was sure I would get them working! I had no money but I guess either people wanted to get rid of their junk, or they saw how young, broke and interested I was, because I ended up with lots of radios. From the components, valves and speakers I collected I was able to get one of the old clunkers working, a multiband shortwave radio in a mahogany cabinet that stood 1.2 m tall. I was fifteen, and soon listening all over the world on my shortwave radio. Radio Australia became one of my favourites.

As my interest in electronics grew, I took a two-year full-time certificate course in electronics and also got my amateur radio licence. While I did my electronics course I worked summers and after school in a local general hardware and gift store. I was 17 years old and the manager, Bruce Allen, in his forties, became a mentor.

Bruce was incredibly energetic, dynamic, witty, and a shrewd businessman. A worldly, big city character trapped in a country town, he seemed determined to make sure I escaped his fate. One day he pulled me aside and said, 'I'm going to teach you all I know about retail because even if you go into electronics, at some stage you're going to have to buy, market and sell something'.

Australia calls

For the next two years Bruce explained about buying products, margins, mark-ups, advertising and sales, and without him having to say a thing about it, I learned a lot about leadership through his own example. He wasn't an office sitter but walked the shop, knew his products, wasn't too proud to do any task at all, and his people would do anything for him.

He knew I wanted to go to Australia, and he encouraged me. My parents understood my desire, and so didn't discourage me. One day I mentioned to Bruce I was having second thoughts about Australia. 'Like *hell* you're not going!' he said. 'You will get on that boat and go. If you don't you will regret it for the rest of your life. You'll always wonder how things would have turned out if you'd gone. Never will you have a better opportunity to go than now, because you're free—no wife, children or mortgage.'

In the early morning of 26 January 1972—sailing day— my train pulled up at the station in Vancouver. I had completed the trans-Canada rail journey, sitting up all the way to save money, with only a few hours to spare and there she was at the dock: the P & O *Orsova*, the largest ship I had ever seen. I didn't know it, but across the Pacific at my destination that very day they had celebrated Australia Day, a public holiday to commemorate the arrival of the First Fleet from England in 1788.

I was shown to E deck, just below the waterline. Nearly all my savings were invested in this passage. The fare was $579, which left me with just over $200. I would have to find work as soon as I arrived. Meanwhile, I would, and did, enjoy a marvellous voyage. I was nineteen.

In Sydney I rented for $10 a week a shabby upstairs room that looked onto a brick wall, sharing the primitive cooking facilities with a couple of mates in the front flat. This choice turned out to be another useful lesson in cost management, for the landlady, known as 'Mrs Mack', was a tough old survivor of the Nazi concentration camps of World War II. She would charge for a second shower a day, reading the electricity meter every morning and charting the consumption hours on a graph.

Our rooms had no heating and we were forbidden to have electric bar heaters, but the cold of an old Sydney terrace house in winter finally led us to break the rules and make the trip to the local Woolworths to splurge on 1000 watt stripheaters. We plugged them in and next morning, feeling a lot warmer, watched over the terrace balcony as Mrs Mack made her daily trip to the meter. There was a shriek of rage, a curse, followed by angry steps up the staircase, the thud of her fist on the door and noisy accusations and abuse. While we were at work that day Mrs Mack came into our rooms and confiscated our heaters—we never saw them again and there was no question of compensation!

My new job was selling tools and automotive accessories at Pauls Hardware, in Sydney's Queen Victoria Building. The historic old building was then in dire need of the major renovation it later got, and diesel exhaust fumes from the busy adjacent bus station continually streamed through the doors of our shop. Three of us worked a long counter, the manager looking down from his office above—he would glare and wave his arms frantically when he saw any social conversation.

My department manager, Noel O'Brien, seemed to take me under his wing. Quietly he advised me not to get caught in a rut working at Pauls. Having a lot of regrets over a career misspent, he would encourage me to do what he had not been able to do—escape before it was too late.

My job with Dick

So, it was no doubt inevitable that the magazine ad for Dick Smith Wholesale that led me and my motorcycle to Dick Smith's little suburban shop a few months later would also lead me to follow up Dick's offer of a job. It seemed he could use a two-way radio technician at Dick Smith Car Radio, his small radio repair centre on the Pacific Highway at North Sydney's Gore Hill. It was mainly patronised by cab drivers needing quick service to get back on the road.

Dick got his service manager to interview me for the job, and at the tail end of the interview Dick walked in. The service manager announced that I would be starting with the company, and that my salary would be $90 a week. Dick gasped, '$90! We can't afford that! The most we can pay is $80.'

I thought how tough he was, considering my salary had just been agreed on with his manager, but the ball was in my court. I took the job. It was October 1972 and I had learned another important lesson: be willing to take a short-term loss for a long-term gain.

Two adjacent buildings housed the fledgling Smith enterprise. One was an old two-storey block of flats, with a small shop in the front. A bedroom in one of the flats above the shop was Dick's office, and at the back was the office of Dawn McCallum, his loyal secretary and bookkeeper. A mixture of stored items, stock and files spilled around the various small rooms in the flats, and it all looked chaotic and disorganised. I worked in the other building, an old factory where car radios, stereos and two-way radios were sold and installed.

My task was to repair the two-way radios and do the occasional installation out in the car park. Lunch time came around and I was chatting to another fellow when he said, 'You know, this place is in receivership'. It soon became apparent to him that I didn't understand what the term meant. 'It means', he said, 'that you have joined a company that's stuffed financially!'

I was horrified: I'd just left my job at Pauls. I recalled Dick's remark that he couldn't afford to pay me $90 a week, and it now made sense. I went home that evening wondering what I had done. Yet, after some serious thought, I decided I was happy: I was now doing what I always dreamed of doing, working with electronics. I went to work next day determined to learn as much as I could while I still held the job, and to enjoy it.

We had a range of regular corporate customers, as well as couriers, truck drivers and a repair contract with ABC Cabs. The cabbies were the most difficult to deal with. Without their radios they were off the road and, being under stress to make a living, they put us under a lot of pressure to get them back on the road. Some would barge into the workshop and stand over you, or impatiently pace up and down while you diagnosed the problem. Occasionally you would be faced with looking for an intermittent fault that wouldn't show up on the bench, so you would have to ride around in the cab until the fault showed up. Sometimes, when you were satisfied you had fixed the problem and had returned to the workshop, you might hear a vehicle charge into the car park and brake heavily, and then a commotion at the front of the building—and you knew you would soon be confronted by one angry, familiar cabbie!

Dick's small electronics shop next door soon took my interest. This had been the Dick Smith Wholesale business I first visited at St Leonards, and he had moved it to Gore Hill so he could keep a closer eye on it. But every time I went into it to collect spare parts for my repairs I would find myself yearning to be back on the sales floor dealing with customers. I could see the frustrations that his retail customers were having in obtaining the things they wanted, because I had the same frustrations. Many of the most common parts I needed were out of stock, and that meant lost sales. I could see that service was slack, the attitude inattentive. What if I could have a job that combined my interests in both retailing and electronics? The opportunity came in a very unexpected way.

Three weeks to prove myself

Dick had invited me home for dinner, and I told him with enthusiasm about my observations, and several other things about how I thought the shop could run better. Dick began to get agitated and finally threw his hands up and exploded, 'Well, why don't you run the bloody place then?'

I lay awake all night thinking about this offer. Next morning I bounced up the stairs to his office and said, 'Dick, I've decided to take the job!' He looked at me blankly. 'What are you talking about?'

'The job running the shop!' I said. He laughed. It was a joke, he said. 'You couldn't do that job, you've got no experience and you're too young.' (I was twenty.)

I set about convincing him to give me a go, saying how I had a technical interest in the products and how I had sold hardware in different places. I also knew by now that Dick liked to do a deal, so as my last card I volunteered to cut my own salary from $80 to $60 a week. His eyes lit up and he said, 'You can do it for three weeks.'

I was determined not to let a great opportunity slip, for I was sure that the shop had the potential to pay me $100 a week. The first thing that needed to be fixed was the shop's appearance. It was filthy, and little thought had been put into merchandising. There was a lot of stock that had been returned by customers under warranty but had not gone back to the suppliers. The staff were grubby and needed to be tidied up.

I began early and I worked until Dick put me out the door each night. The three-week trial period went by and he said nothing, and as it extended into six weeks I was feeling more confident.

'Well, Dick,' I finally said, 'how am I going?'

His reply was brief. 'Good! I'm putting you up to $100 a week.'

Chapter 2
Building Dick Smith Electronics

When by mid-1973 the business began to grow, I had got to know Dick better. He was eight years older than I was but he treated me as an equal, and I responded to it. I now knew why his little electronics shop had gone into receivership: $18 000 worth of inventory had been stolen. He was paying back all his creditors, and his sincerity and honesty impressed me. I also sensed that he was a person who would be successful because he seemed to make logical decisions. More often than not I agreed with his commonsense approach to things. Having, as a teenager, pored over copies of America's Lafayette and Allied Radio electronics catalogues, I also liked the catalogue he had produced that year, and his mail-order business seemed to have potential.

As in any small business, you had to do something of everything, so I did some of the buying, served customers, took delivery of shipments and, in any spare time, filled mail-orders and packed them. Most of our suppliers still wanted to be paid cash before they would deliver to us, but the quantities we bought were increasing. Not that we were flush with funds.

The Dick Smith 1973 catalogue was a big success and Dick had it printed and stapled into the leading electronics magazine so that most of the keen hobbyists got a copy. On Saturday mornings there was a small crowd outside the little shop waiting to get in. Dick had put a price on the catalogue with some redeemable coupons inside, so if you spent a certain amount you got the price of the catalogue back. We began selling more catalogues than any other product. We were out of receivership now and it became obvious that the business was going to be successful.

One day that year Dick invited me up to his office for a talk. 'Ike,' he said, 'the company's doing well—our sales for the week were $10 000. I'd like to do something for you. From now on you can have free petrol on the company account.' Well, I came down the stairs beaming at this news—although I didn't own a car, only a motorcycle, and it cost me just 50 cents to fill that up. And, furthermore, I *walked* to work! Don't laugh. The fact is I felt appreciated. Here was a real businessman I would continue to learn *heaps* from. The lesson: making your people feel special needn't cost a lot of money.

Dick's face becomes his trademark

Dick's face was becoming famous as his business trade-mark. In house we referred to it as the 'Dickhead'. A man named Neville Corbett had come into the car radio business one day to have some repairs done and Dick, while working on his car, asked him what he did for a living. Dick often asked this question of customers. Neville said he

DICK SMITH

CAR RADIO "NUT"

Nork fawned thel imination convatipons hame menow gome inial tectinical throle rung benteen wairdrie ban crenty induted recvo chet butrexey popmar wite thule Teh darip perty dma teh du flete, tato tine mone thand wenon smot hotly ad alnot tham, howver, weas ont wa thertir lasrtime hotwitu apc A proshion scof alth lepes sed Gow lasdung

DICK SMITH CAR RADIO
162 PACIFIC HIGHWAY GORE HILL
Phone 43 5530, 43 3449

'It's fantastic!' Dick's first ad, gobbledygook included.

was an advertising agent, but Dick didn't know just what that was. Neville explained that he designed ads for companies, and Dick said, 'Well, I need an advertising agent. I want to become famous around Sydney as the car-radio expert and you can call me a radio nut. But I've got no more than $120 a week to spend on advertising.'

Next day the agent sent a photographer to take Dick's picture, and a few days later he turned up with the draft ad.

DICK SMITH

CAR THIEF BOFFIN

Next time your car is stolen rush in to Dick Smith. Have him explain how his burglar alarm would have saved the loss.
Don't act now! Your car may never be stolen.

DICK SMITH ELECTRONICS
162 PACIFIC HIGHWAY
GORE HILL
Phone 43 5530, 43 3449

DICK SMITH

BENDS OVER BACKWARDS

Dick really is 'nutty' about car radios and he's the only dealer that bends over backwards to give you a better deal. What a fanatic! Watch Dick in action . . . a real scream! Go on, take advantage of the poor boy's condition . . . everyone else is.

DICK SMITH CAR RADIO
162 PACIFIC HIGHWAY
GORE HILL
Phone 43 5530, 43 3449

DICK SMITH

HOW DOES DICK LOOK IN STEREO?

—much the same. It's those glasses we guess! Anyway, Dick Smith is in car stereo in the biggest way, goggles and all. He's a bit carried away, but that's to your good because you'll get your 8-tracker installed quicker, better and cheaper. Biggest range of pre-recorded tapes, too.

DICK SMITH ELECTRONICS
162 PACIFIC HIGHWAY
GORE HILL
Phone 43 5530, 43 3449

The message would change, but the 'Dickhead' was here to stay.

They had reversed Dick's face onto a bromide, resulting in the now famous Dick Smith logo. The headline said, 'Dick Smith, Car Radio Nut!' and at the bottom of the ad was our address, 162 Pacific Highway, Gore Hill. In between there was a slab of text in meaningless gobbledygook, of the sort that ad designers lay down for positional purposes and to indicate type size and style.

Dick looked at the ad and yelled, 'It's fantastic! It's brilliant!'

'But you haven't read the text yet!' said Neville, handing him a separate sheet with it on. Dick was only momentarily surprised. 'Never mind', he said. 'I want it to run like *that*.'

So they ran it in the daily paper regularly and people would drive from far-off suburbs past other car-radio installers who were more experienced than we were, to give their business to the nice but nutty car-radio enthusiast with the crazy ad.

Goodbye, car radios

Dick himself is a very competent technician, but finding good employees was difficult and there was one entire, unbelievable week in 1973 that was probably the catalyst for Dick making the final decision to get out of the car-radio business and focus on the growing electronics shop I was managing.

One of the procedures he insisted on in the radio business was that the customer leave the car when we were doing a radio installation, but one Monday a customer wanted to stay in his car. The radio installer inadvertently drilled through the heater coil and a powerful jet of hot water scalded the man's foot and he ended in hospital.

On Tuesday a fellow drove in with a car that had hydrolastic suspension. While the installer was drilling a hole for the rear speaker he cut into the hydrolastic line and the car's suspension collapsed. A tow truck had to be called to get the car out of the building.

On Wednesday Dick had trouble with a young employee who, despite being under driving age, sneaked every opportunity to drive cars in and out of the building. Dick caught him backing out a car, ordered him out of the driver's seat, jumped in and quickly reversed it himself. When he applied the brakes at the edge of the pavement nothing happened, and the car sped backwards right across busy Pacific Highway to the other side of the road. Only luck saved him from catastrophe. The installer had bored into the brake line and the brake fluid was expelled when the brake was depressed.

Dick must have thought things couldn't continue like this, but they did. He had repeatedly told one of the installers that when drilling a hole to mount the aerial on the roof he had to place a metal plate above the roof lining so the drill wouldn't penetrate the lining. Dick happened to walk by on the Thursday just as the installer's drill went through the roof lining of a luxury car, ripping it badly, and then picked up the rear-vision mirror and wrecked that.

And on the Friday? Dick had always made it clear that when they were drilling holes under the dash the installers had to pull the wiring loom away to prevent any damage. On Friday a customer, with his new radio installed, drove a kilometre or two before turning on his headlights, only to have the car fill with smoke. The installer had shorted out the wiring loom, and the whole car had to be rewired.

But before Dick took the important step of selling his car-radio business, he flew to the United States and the United Kingdom to look at the big electronic retailers such as Lafayette, Allied Radio, Radio Shack, Olsen Electronics and Laskys. What he did there was what we did in a dozen different ways in later years: he learned from our rivals. Whenever we wanted to go into something new we researched the market to see what others had done. Dick took the commonsense view that it was a waste of time and resources to invent the wheel when somebody had already done it. We, after all, were new to electronics retailing, but these companies had had years of solid experience.

Dick came home with a notepad full of ideas that he immediately put into practice. So, we became the first electronics retailer in Australia to sell components in self-serve display bins, and to carpet our store. We adopted lighting and colour schemes that Dick had seen overseas. By 1974 we had a sales turnover of more than $2 million from our shop at Gore Hill, and we never looked back. That year we opened two new stores, in Bankstown and York Street in the city. I was made general manager in 1975 at the age of twenty-three, which raised a few eyebrows when outsiders asked to see the GM. By April 1976 we had five stores, but it was still only the beginning of Dick Smith Electronics' business success, as you can see from the timeline on pages 96–102.

Meeting Tandy head on

Almost from the beginning, Dick's genuine pride in being Australian was a key factor in his business philosophy, but he made it a public issue in 1975, when the American giant Tandy Electronics came to Australia and opened a store in York Street, a few doors from our city store. You can imagine how disappointed we were to have paid all our debts and come out of receivership, with all the stress and hard work that had involved, only to be confronted by a powerful company with apparently unlimited funds to establish themselves in Australia.

In our roneoed staff newsletter Dick warned the staff:

> Within the next year we will be facing very severe competition from Tandy. In fact I predict that by the end of 1976 Tandy will have at least 120 stores throughout Australia ... They are prepared to operate for a period of five years at a financial loss to set up in Australia. No Australian organisation could possibly do this because the financial resources required are enormous. How many firms could continue to operate after a loss of nearly a half-million dollars in the first year? Could any Australian firm spend $250 000 to let themselves be known? This is not free enterprise, it is not competition, it is totally unfair. Tandy's aim in Australia is to force all small businessmen from their market. In the US, this method of competing is more difficult because there is still substantial competition, and financially it is nearly impossible.

Tandy deserve their growth and success after operating for forty years in their own country. But why should a foreign firm be allowed by the Australian Government to take over the Australian market from the Australian people and remain 99 per cent foreign-owned?

Is the general public aware of this future development? I doubt it. Will the Australian Government protect our business from foreign takeover? I doubt it. It is up to us to do something now before we are 'Yanked' out of business!

What Dick did was, literally, to take to the streets.

We organised a staff demonstration outside Tandy's York Street store. Inside that evening their managing director, Dean Lawrence, whom Dick and I quite liked, was launching a new profit-sharing scheme for their managers. Our

We take to the streets outside Tandy's city store in 1975.

staff turned out with placards declaring 'Go Home Yanks!' and made such a commotion on the street that it drowned out their meeting. A police van arrived, and so did television crews, press and radio. The story of our concern about being squeezed to death by American big business got a great run in the media and made us the Australian underdogs, attracting a lot of customer support.

We helped the mood by promoting our 100 per cent Aussie ownership, and the fact that our profits stayed here. I organised a badge—'Australian Owned and Proud of It'—that all the staff wore. We began to fly the Australian flag outside our shops, and at our busy Gore Hill outlet we raised a large 10 m banner that read, 'Proud To Be Australian'. Many years later Dick would use the 'Australian owned, profits stay here' principle to enter the food business with Dick Smith Foods.

Of course, we still had to be competitive with our products. We made sure we used our local knowledge about what hobbyists and electronic consumers wanted to advantage. We also made sure we got that knowledge long before Tandy's global managers in Fort Worth, Texas.

It was certainly unfortunate for Tandy that their house brand was 'RS', which stood for Radio Shack, the parent company's chain of stores in the United States. In Australia, RS had a slang connotation: 'ratshit'. (I didn't know at the time that Dick, at the age of eighteen, had registered the business name RS Electronics—RS for Richard Smith—to start his own business.) The Tandy RS brand became a bit of a joke, but fortunately Tandy did many other things

This picture of our Gore Hill shop in 1976 was put on sale in the United Kingdom as a postcard without reference to us, so I can't say whether the point of the photographer's interest was the patriotic banner or the heated toilet seats.

wrong, especially by following US market trends too closely. In 1976 we began to feel more confident when Tandy reported a loss for the year of $686 000 and we had made a profit of $709 000. It was unfortunate for Tandy, too, that their founder, chairman and CEO, Charles Tandy, died in 1978. Anyway, they didn't become a serious danger to us, because our local knowledge of the Australian marketplace gave us an edge.

In 2001, Dick Smith Electronics, then owned by Woolworths, purchased all Tandy's Australian operations.

Chapter 3

Riding high on
the electronics boom

By 1976, after the enormous success of the three Sydney stores, we decided we would tackle the interstate market in Melbourne and Brisbane. We already had a huge following of mail-order customers itching to buy from us in person and our new shops were packed on opening days. We had big problems, though, trying to find good, dependable employees at such a distance from head office, and during the first few years I spent an incredible amount of time setting up the ground rules for running a business at arm's length. We decided that all our shops should be clones: all would stock the same products and be run under the same disciplined guidelines we set.

We made everything as simple as possible for the management of a store. We purchased everything, housed it in our Sydney warehouse and shipped it to the stores with the selling price stamped on every item. Sometimes we might buy a product in Melbourne yet we still shipped it to Sydney and back to Melbourne just to keep things simple for store management. The important thing was that our people be focused on customer service, and we didn't expect to uncover many good salespeople who were also good buyers and good business managers.

Our sales staff were incredibly young, their ages averaging from fifteen to twenty-one at different shops. I was in my early twenties and managing a lot of young people could be challenging at times, as I had to play the role of foster parent to some of them, but I enjoyed it all, and I was learning too. We were all part of an exciting, dynamic new technological boom. Our business attracted Australia's young hobbyists, who became our main source of recruits, and the company was highly energised by their youthful exuberance. We put notices in our catalogue to say we were always looking for 'really keen enthusiasts to come and help us maintain and improve our mail-order business ... So if you build the projects, read the catalogue from cover to cover and know what it's all about, how about dropping us a line? If you live out of town come in for a six month working holiday. We'll even find you somewhere to live!' For them it was like working in an Aladdin's treasure cave—and it was a great place to make friends and learn about business. Many of them later used the experience to start their own businesses.

The great CB radio fad

It was the citizen's band radio fad that really gave us an amazing boost in profit. This is best demonstrated by the tale of our office IBM System 32, which we had had installed to track our inventory and gross profit. One morning when we came to work the computer had gone berserk. Dick leapt on the phone and told IBM just what he thought of their system, and to 'get up here quick!' They came up quick, and they found the problem was that one of our products had made too much profit. They reminded us that before they installed the system they had set its parameters after asking whether we would ever make more than \$100 000 gross profit on any single product in one month, and Dick had yelled out, 'Never!' But that month one of our CB radios, the Hygain V, had grossed \$120 000.

The great CB radio fad also gave us some other, more serious, problems. There was an interesting debate about CB radios going on at that time, because you had to have a special amateur radio licence to operate one legally. Yet it was not illegal to buy one. This anomaly was very attractive to young people, especially to young males, who were buying the radios because they could do something illegal with them and thus join the adventurous ranks of 'pirates'. CB radio clubs were formed all over the country and users had their own language, which included 'handles' (fake names), and 'eyeballs' (meetings with other operators at secret locations). There were an estimated 175 000 operators in Australia in 1977. It was a completely harmless rebellion against petty authority, and there was wide support in the community for the elimination of the outdated licensing system. With his usual ebullience, Dick set himself the task of lobbying the Commonwealth government to legalise CB use for everyone, without the need for licences. It brought him a lot of attention.

He won the battle, but then we almost lost the war. The moment use of CB radios was legalised, people lost interest. It wasn't necessary now for them to hit the big switch and hide their microphone between their knees when a patrol car from the Commonwealth Department of Communications came into view. We had taken all the fun out of it! It was one of our biggest blunders. CB radio sales plummeted overnight, and we were left with $900 000

When Dick sought to promote his *CB Radio Handbook* on Jimmy Hannan's radio show, he couldn't get an interview, so without informing Hannan he cheekily ran this ad in the afternoon newspapers. He got his interview.

worth of stock in our warehouse—a huge amount for a company our size. We were even concerned that our folly might send us under. Of course, we were not the only business affected by the CB collapse, and a number of companies did go broke. Fortunately, because of our conservative financial policies, we didn't owe a cent on our mountain of unsold CB radios and, over time, we sold all of them, and at the full profit margin. We emerged still the Number 1 CB radio retailer.

Expanding the company

Dick was becoming less involved with the day-to-day running of the company, which was to be expected as he took on more and more flying and adventuring, but I enjoyed the excitement of a growing business, and I admit that when the pace was especially rapid I even liked the feeling of it being 'almost out of control'. Whenever things got organised and appeared to be settling down, I got bored. I saw opportunities for expansion but Dick, having once been in receivership, wasn't keen to take on more financial risk. He would say, 'Look, Ike, because I own the company I could lose everything if we go broke, but you can just walk away and get another job'. He was right, of course. He was sole owner, it was his capital, his risk, and I understood his view. Not that it deterred me, or other ambitious managers, from pressuring him.

I knew the only way I was going to make more money was to manage a larger company. I wanted to open in Adelaide. I had a building in mind but the lease, as usual, required Dick personally to guarantee the rent for the term. Dick said he refused to sign another lease for a shop, so I went to the owner and explained the difficulty. Could we sign the lease without Dick having to guarantee it personally? He agreed, and from then on all the leases I negotiated had this clause struck out. Furthermore, we added a clause to say we wanted an option to purchase the site at the end of the lease, and to my surprise all our landlords agreed. I don't think they thought our small electronics retail company could ever afford to buy their properties, but because the business was in an even stronger cash position when the leases expired we ended up owning many of the shops.

Fine-tuning the retail formula

We were gradually fine-tuning our retail formula. I found a very competent sales trainer, Graham Foster, who helped us inject professionalism into sales and service in the stores, and a very good retail manager, Stephen Downes. The business was an exciting place, and I loved my job. I thought that working with someone like Dick was a unique experience, to enjoy as long as I could, but I could tell that Dick was worrying about his personal risks in the business, and when in 1978 he held talks with Winchcombe Carson about buying Dick Smith Electronics, I wasn't surprised and could empathise with him. He had enough money to do the things he had dreamed of and he also wanted to spend more time with his family. The business adventure for Dick was ending and he wanted to begin the next adventure, but the sale fell through.

This was also the year we bought Audio Bar, a chain of nine concessions operating in the nine Grace Bros department stores in Sydney. We expanded them by adding our exclusive products. Buying these concessions was a great learning experience, because although they were profitable they were a logistics nightmare to operate. They all had to have reliable managers, all had to be supplied from our warehouse and all had to operate under tight controls, so I was constantly on the road supervising them. Finally, I said to Dick, 'This is crazy. There's as much work in managing these small-turnover outlets as there is in one of our larger company-owned stores with ten times the turnover. Why don't we shut them down and open our own stores?' He agreed and, even though they were profitable, we closed them.

It was 1979 and we were now in our large, purpose-built, much more efficient headquarters at North Ryde, Sydney, complete with the largest flag in Australia, which could be seen for kilometres and was a guaranteed talking point. It also had a helipad that Dick flew in and out of in his newly acquired Bell JetRanger. We were purchasing more and more from Hong Kong, in the late 1970s an electronics Mecca and a popular destination for Australian tourists because of its duty-free shopping. Dick thought that as we visited it so often we should open a permanent buying-office, together with a duty-free shop directed at the tourists. The shop opened close to the popular Ned Kelly's bar and the customers liked it because we would

The largest flag in Australia, on the highest flagpole, got plenty of free publicity when Dick raised it at Sydney headquarters ...

… and made even more of a flap when it was stolen a few months later.

honour product guarantees back in Australia, but because dramas seemed to arise regularly we spent an enormous amount of our management time there—and we got no more new products than we had been picking up on our regular visits. I think if we'd been able to find the right senior manager it would have worked well, but when we looked at its first year of operation we'd made just $50 000 net profit. It simply wasn't worth the investment of our time. We closed it, our earlier experience that management time should be spent where it gains you the greatest profit return having been reinforced.

The advancement of the silicon chip was rapidly spawning a myriad of new products, many at much lower prices and with features unimagined just a few years earlier. Two products were to add enormously to the success of the business: one was a video computer game called the Dick Smith Wizard, the other a personal computer that we called the Dick Smith System 80.

Woolworths takes a major shareholding

Meanwhile, Ted Perry, who had introduced us to Winchcombe Carson, at Dick's suggestion came up with a list of Australian companies that could be interested in buying Dick Smith Electronics. Woolworths was one of the names on the list and in 1980 they agreed to acquire 60 per cent of the business and Dick had an option to sell the remaining 40 per cent at the end of two years. Thus he reduced some of his risk.

I was excited to be part of a large company that wanted to grow larger, but I knew that Dick Smith Electronics would never be quite the same again—and it never was. There would be board meetings to attend, head office management meetings, corporate plans, budgeting, the trade unions—all things I had not had anything to do with—and at times I didn't want to be part of such a formal hierarchical culture. Yet the Woolworths people were wonderful to work with, very supportive, and they loved our business and the profit it was making. I got along very well with the chairman, Sir Eric McClintock, and the managing director, Tony Harding.

Tandy Electronics had developed the best selling TRS-80, the first mass-produced home personal computer. Our Dick Smith System 80 was made in Hong Kong by a very clever company called EACA. They used the TRS-80 as a benchmark design, with the same BASIC operating language and the Z80 microprocessor, which ran at the amazing speed of 1.7 MHz. Because the software Tandy had developed worked on our computer there was already a huge number of useable programs on the market. With some help from us, EACA developed additional features so the machine would be more competitive. For example, ours could operate using any television set as a monitor, so you didn't have to buy a monitor. The basic model came with only 4 K of memory and sold for $695, but this was about $200 cheaper than Tandy's. We sold a staggering 12 500 of this enormously successful computer over two years. Why Tandy never retaliated surprised us, but perhaps they had no idea how many we were selling.

Dick was surprised and intrigued by the demand for personal computers, for he thought they were useless. He would ask somebody what a computer could be used for and they might say, 'To store your recipes' or 'To balance your cheque book'. His blunt reply was, 'Well, why don't you keep all your bloody recipes in an index box, and balance your cheque book against your bank statement!' If you compare computers then with later machines, he had a point. The real users at that time were hobbyists trying out something new, and young people who wanted to play games. I was a real enthusiast because I had seen prototypes at the Las Vegas consumer electronics fairs in the 1970s— including the first Apple, which would later captivate the world—but Dick, in his cheerfully forthright way, would tell interviewing journalists that the computer was 'absolutely useless' and he couldn't understand why anybody would want to buy one. 'Then why are you selling them?' they would ask. And his reply was, 'Because I can sell them cheaper and you waste less of your money.'

Between 1980 and 1982, with these products booming, I pushed to expand the business. With Woolworths' shareholding, the shackles on growth had been removed and in the next two years we virtually doubled the number of stores, our sales and our net profit. I knew, though, that our growth was going to be more challenging in the future. All the major population centres now had a Dick Smith store. I wanted to try an offshore shop, with my final ambition being to take on Tandy on their home turf. So why not experiment in a country closer to home? New Zealand.

Dick Smith Electronics goes into New Zealand

The idea of operating in New Zealand was one thing, getting permission to operate there was another matter. The country had an archaic licensing system for imported goods, many of the licences having been issued in the 1930s and 1940s. The system was meant to protect local industry, but it appeared that the privileged few who held import licences were free to charge just about anything they wanted, so the system merely protected profits.

Dick and I flew to Auckland in May 1980 to drum up some publicity that might turn the tide. On talk-back radio the local response was overwhelmingly in favour of us trying to break down the barriers. Dick enjoyed the controversy. Consumers were fed up with protectionism that resulted in them paying up to three or four times the price they should. The system was eventually changed and we were allowed to bring some of our product range into New Zealand. Not that this especially gratified Dick, who continued stirring government and the competition with his usual direct, simply–tell–it–like–it–is announcements, such as this one:

> *Dear New Zealand Customers.* I should be overjoyed to think that I've finally opened a branch in New Zealand. After all, it's an aim I've worked towards for many years. The fact is, I'm a little sad about it. Why? My company has been able to offer New Zealanders only about 25% of our total catalogue range! Yes, my prices are up to 60% lower than the prices you've been forced to pay, but the simple fact is that we're not allowed to offer you similar savings on the other 75% of our

lines. We would dearly love to offer you all the electronic goodies we sell back in Australia—but we cannot. So New Zealanders are paying higher prices than Australian enthusiasts—mostly because there is so little competition. This is ridiculous. Why should you pay such exorbitant prices?

You must know about the 'licensing' system of importing goods into New Zealand. The privileged few who have these licences can charge just about whatever they like—mostly because there is very little competition on these products. The usual reason given is 'to protect New Zealand jobs ...' This is patently absurd—if items are being imported under the licensing system, all that is being protected is huge profits for the licensees. The Government doesn't benefit. The New Zealand people obviously don't benefit. So where is the point in having these restrictive licences? By the way, the licensing system doesn't apply in reverse—a New Zealand electronics company opened up in Australia selling freely and openly, with some items selling for around 30% of the price back 'home'. Isn't that amazing?

We have found that by opening our store in New Zealand, local prices have mysteriously dropped. Therefore, even if you choose not to shop at Dick Smith Electronics, you should still end up paying less for your components. And I'm sure you'll agree, that's good for all New Zealanders. It's over to you. *Dick Smith*

With the few lines we could import, I had estimated we would do $300 000 in sales and break even in our first year operating in New Zealand (1981–82), but we actually made $300 000 in profit.

Dick decided to sell the remaining 40 per cent of his business in 1982. I was expecting it, for he was planning a big new adventure—to be the first to fly a helicopter solo around the world—and he was spending a lot of time preparing for the challenge. It was time for me, too, to consider my future. I knew I would miss Dick's management style, the rapport and friendship we had built up in the many years we had worked together. I was also beginning to be concerned by the problems then facing Woolworths, who were losing market share of their core business to opposition Coles and battling rising costs.

But our business was booming in July 1982 as Dick sold his remaining interests in Dick Smith Electronics. Sales had risen 45 per cent for the year, and in less than two years the number of stores had grown from fourteen to thirty-three, including one in New Zealand. One morning Dick bounced into my office and said, 'Ike, I intend to book the Concert Hall at the Opera House and thank everyone for their help in building the company'.

We invited around 2000 people. They included early customers, employees, suppliers and very special friends, such as Noel O'Brien, my old boss at Pauls Hardware who had warned me years earlier not to get caught in a rut there. The Concert Hall was packed and the atmosphere exciting. There was great entertainment, and Dick gave a very warm and grateful speech. It was rewarding moments like these that made working with Dick very special.

In any case, I had good reason to recall the start of that evening, when my wife Louise and I were given the honour of escorting New South Wales Premier Neville Wran and his wife, Jill, to their seats. I had bought a new suit for the occasion only that day, and as we led the Wrans up the Opera House steps, I was one of the few in the party unaware that a sale price tag, 'WAS $299, *NOW* $199' was hanging from my coat-tail. Not until I reached the top of the steps did I get a whisper from one of our managers, 'You got a fantastic deal on that suit!', as he ripped the ticket off.

And on to the United States

I needed a new challenge, so Woolworths agreed to let me go to the United States for two years and establish Dick Smith in California. This would enable us to investigate our chances of tapping into the wider United States market, and if it didn't look like working out we could close it down. Meanwhile, it would be challenging and fun.

I decided against the expense of starting a business from scratch—I thought it best to buy into a local company and use their local knowledge. The ideal business was Jameco Electronics, a very profitable mail-order company to which we could add a retail presence. The owner was Dennis Farrey. I had come across his catalogue while attending an electronics trade show in Las Vegas and decided to drop in on him.

We found we had immediate rapport. Dennis's father had died when he was sixteen and he had left a small Midwest town to seek a job in California so he could support his family. His first job was in a wholesale grocery distribution business, where he learned the basics of dealing that enabled him to establish a business in semi-conductors, buying and storing them in huge quantities when they were cheap. Later, when the computer manufacturers down the freeway to Silicon Valley were screaming for stock and prices went sky-high, he made a fortune. One Christmas Dennis gave the fellow who taught him everything in the grocery business a new Mercedes Benz as a thank-you. That was the type of man he was.

When he showed me around his company it was obvious from the atmosphere that this was a well-run business. There was an exciting air of enthusiasm and efficiency. He did all his business through the mail-order catalogue. I suggested to Dennis that we buy his business. He would run it and teach us about the United States market and we would help him set up retail stores.

Dennis was only half-interested, yet interested enough to fly to Sydney to look at our operations. We had a round of meetings with Woolworths, and I gave him the grand tour of Woolies and Dick Smith shops. He was warming to the idea, but I suspected he was too much of a maverick, someone who coveted the freedom of running his own business and not having to report to anyone. I understood that attitude very well from my own experience.

Dennis decided to retain his freedom and we decided we would open a Dick Smith branch in the United States ourselves. I was in charge of the launch. It made sense to open in Silicon Valley, but embarrassingly the only suitable building we found was just down the road from Dennis's! I felt uneasy about this and was still disappointed that we hadn't done the deal with him, because our entry through

Jameco Electronics would have put us in the black from day one.

Soon after we opened in Silicon Valley, Redwood City, in 1985, I took a phone call from Dennis. He asked how I was fitting in, how business was, and what I thought of America. Five minutes after I hung up there was a man outside my office with a huge package. With a big smile, he yelled out: 'I'm from Jameco Electronics and Dennis said to give you this.'

The package contained a massive printout, with the names and addresses of every customer on Jameco Electronics' California mailing list: all 180 000 of them! He had just given us an amazing start in the American market. Scrawled across the printout in Dennis's handwriting were words I shall never forget: 'Welcome to America. This is the best gift I could ever give you. Good luck with your venture! – Dennis'.

Teaser ads we ran to introduce Electronic Dick to California.

I demonstrate to our US customers—as best I can—the elusive principles of the 'beer-powered radio'. We invented it back home, but the Yanks loved it too.

Within twelve months we had four stores open and mail-order customers all over North America, including Boeing, AT&T, IBM and hundreds of schools, universities and colleges, and lots of US government agencies. We even supplied the builders of the space shuttle rocket booster (and were relieved a component of ours wasn't involved in the loss of the ill-fated Challenger that year). We had three front covers on the leading electronics magazine, *Radio Electronics*, dedicated to our exclusive electronics kits. One of our radio receiver kits was featured in a Merit Badge Book published by the Boy Scouts of America and our staff were excited that every Boy Scout who built our kit would get a Merit Badge.

In this US ad we joyfully sent up the opposition Tandy Electronics' Radio Shack stores.

The Americans liked us. Paul Hogan had done a brilliant job promoting Australia and this paved the way for us to get lots of attention ourselves. I had fantastic staff, the four Australians I took over worked harder than I have ever seen people work, and the local American employees were incredibly dedicated. Our stores' average sales were as good as Radio Shack's. All we had to do was open more outlets to spread the overheads. I knew we would make money within three years if we could keep the operation supported. I had made it clear that I wanted to spend only two years in the United States, but Woolworths wanted me to stay longer and I might have, if there had not been unexpected developments.

Dick Smith reappears

Back in Australia, 1986 wasn't a good year for Woolworths. Profit for the first half was down 89 per cent to a mere $2.6 million on sales of $2.6 billion. When I heard this I knew there would be little chance of funds for our expansion. To cap it, Woolworths announced in October 1986 that as part of its rationalisation program it planned to sell the entire Dick Smith Electronics group. I wasn't excited by the prospect of going through another sale.

I also longed to be back in Australia. I would wake every morning to the news from Radio Australia on our short-wave radio. I missed all things Australian—the people, our culture—and my heart was in Australia. I loved our way of life and I wanted our newly born son to grow up there.

It was a telephone call from Dick Smith in late 1986 that was the catalyst. He suggested we work together again at Australian Geographic, which he had successfully launched in January that year after eighteen months of hard work. My immediate answer was that I didn't know a thing about publishing. To which he replied, 'But neither do I!' Minutes later a deal had been done.

I agreed to start on half the salary I was then getting and to stay a minimum of twelve months. It wasn't the first time that I took a short-term loss for a long-term gain with Dick, and I would learn about a new industry and again have the excitement of helping to build a new company, and in Australia. The old team was back in a new adventure.

Chapter 4
The 'unbelievable' Australian Geographic

The quarterly *Australian Geographic* had just made publishing history as the most successful launch ever of an Australian magazine. In California I had received a telex from Dick, dated 1 January 1986, reading, 'Unbelievable. Unbelievable. Unbelievable ... first issue sold out in newsagents in days, now 21 000 subscribers. Reprinting 30 000, to make 110 000 in total.' Within a few months the journal had 60 000 paid-up subscribers and, with my airmail subscription, I was familiar with its glossy pages. My reaction was that here was a great magazine with enormous potential to sell nature-related products to its readers. I loved the outdoors and had discovered a shop at the Stanford Shopping Center in Palo Alto, where we lived, called The Nature Company. Filled with nature-related products, such as wildlife-themed gifts, camping and bushwalking equipment, it had a captivating, natural feel: it was a magical shop. I did not suspect then that in May 1987 I would be behind a desk in Sydney as Australian Geographic's CEO.

I was happy to be back working with Dick. It was also a relief to be quit of all the paperwork, board meetings and other formalities of a big public company. Here I could just get on with running the business. Dick and I had built up a mutual trust over the years; we didn't have to communicate all the time—we just pursued what we wanted to do. For several reasons, I knew this would be an interesting, unusual year. That January Dick had been named 1987 Australian of the Year and he would have to embark on many speaking tours around the country in the next few months. In his acceptance speech he had said he wanted to see Australia's wealthiest putting something back into the country, and he encouraged them all to take a year off from making money and do it. He also said his own major goal for the year was to reduce the number of 15-year-olds who smoked cigarettes (32 per cent). While he had nothing against people smoking, he opposed the cigarette company ads he believed were being directed at youth. (In 1989 his efforts were rewarded when the Senate approved a Bill banning cigarette advertising in newspapers and magazines.)

A new industry

One of my first tasks was to learn the business and I spent the first few months observing, talking to people and finding out as much as I could about an industry quite new to me. Dick was becoming frustrated with the management issues that most start-up companies have. One problem was finding good journalists who agreed philosophically with what he had set out to do: basically, to produce positive, inspirational, factually accurate stories about Australia. The business also had some personnel problems that were affecting morale. In any new company some of the wrong people get hired, for there is not a refined formula to follow, and this results in mavericks with personal agendas attempting to set things up the way they want them. There can be chaotic bickering and jostling for position, favour and reward.

To make Dick's situation worse, my arrival coincided with the publication in the *Sydney Morning Herald* that May of a story headed, 'Magazine Turns Sour for Dick Smith', which had a devastating effect on Dick's own morale because of its serious inaccuracies. I found him about ready to toss it all in. To refute the article, he had invited the Fairfax people in to look at his files, but with the ponderous schedule surrounding these things it was months before he extracted written apologies from both the *Herald* and the writer of the story. The writer wrote that he 'regretted that the article appeared in its published form and for not having checked the facts fully before submitting it for publication'.

The goals are set for expansion

Despite the start–up pains, the staff had done a first-rate job on *Australian Geographic* and I became even more excited by the prospects of expanding the business. The readers were incredibly enthused and loyal; what we had to do was get some more good people, plan and organise ourselves better, and develop an enthusiastic team spirit. In June 1987 I wrote a memo about our goals, and sent a copy to Dick.

The main goals were to get the journal to 200 000 subscribers (there were then around 100 000), and the subscription renewal rate up from 66 per cent to 75–80 per cent, to have the best staff—people Dick would be happy with—and to produce the best maps possible. I added at the very bottom of the page a message to Dick, 'After all of this is done and you are happy, let's sell nature products by mail-order, and possibly later through retail outlets, and do a DSE again'.

I didn't get a reply to that, but the seed had been planted for future discussion. I knew that convincing Dick to 'do a DSE' again would not be easy. It would mean financial risk, more employees, warehousing, inventories—all the details that had resulted in Dick getting out of retail.

This time around, working at Australian Geographic, was certainly different from those early days at Dick Smith Electronics. Instead of being in receivership with run-down buildings and second-hand furniture, and insufficient money to do the things we wanted to do, we were working in the midst of a magnificent, landscaped wildlife sanctuary that Dick had created on four hectares of land near his home at Terrey Hills, north of the city. Brand new buildings had been designed so the bush and animals were in sight from everyone's offices. Wallabies and emus would inquisitively peer in at you through the floor-to-ceiling glass, and it was common for visitors to my office to completely lose their train of thought as a territorial black swan chased after a wood duck on the pond or a couple of emus suddenly began a mad and entertaining game of hide-and-seek. Frogs croaked among the reeds in surrounding pools,

The Australian Geographic Centre: 'paradise to work in'.

possums scrambled across ceilings and birds abounded amid the native habitat, with the shrubs and trees labelled with their botanical details. It was a paradise within which to work on 'Dick Smith's journal of discovery and adventure', as our front cover had it.

This time around, Dick too was different. He had made enough money and he would say to me, 'I'm not motivated to build another business. I want to put something back into the country and do things that give me satisfaction.' He had announced in the first issue that he would guarantee at least $100 000 in support every year to Australian Geographic's Scientific Research and Expedition Fund. This was no problem for me as far as my own objectives were concerned. We could both do something towards these new goals. If I helped expand the business we would make more profit to put towards Dick's aims of supporting scientific research, adventure and other worthy causes.

The *Australian Encyclopaedia* and our first calendar

On my desk when I arrived was a note from Dick asking me to look into the possible purchase of the rights to the *Australian Encyclopaedia*. This multi-volume reference work had first been published by the founder of Angus & Robertson, George Robertson, in 1925. In the 1950s it had been sold to the American-owned company Grolier Society, and later bought by a New Zealand firm, David Bateman Ltd. As a boy Dick thought himself lucky to have been given four volumes of the ten volume edition, a broken set his father happened to acquire. Dick told me that he would sit on the floor in front of the radiogram poring over those odd volumes, dreaming of travel and adventure, and it was what he found in them that kindled his early love of the country.

David Bateman was looking for sponsorship to produce a new edition but, as it was owned overseas, instead of sponsoring it Dick decided we should buy it and bring it back to Australian ownership. We added lots of new entries and we doubled the selling price because Grolier told me they had been struggling with the costs, which was why they had sold it. We printed 10 000 sets and launched it from beside the historic Tank Stream, colonial Sydney's first water supply, hidden but still running beneath the streets of the city. This created a lot of publicity. Our new edition was an outstanding success, with 5000 sets at $595 a set being sold in a few months.

That year, 1988, we also launched the *Australian Geographic* calendar. I had seen the large Audubon Society bird calendar and had learned that a calendar was a top-selling product with *National Geographic*'s readers. I worked out the selling price we would have to set if we were to make a reasonable profit on a very large format (500 × 433 mm) calendar with fine art reproduction prints for every month, and it came to $22.95 including postage. A lot of people I spoke to about it laughed, saying nobody would pay that much for a huge and heavy calendar they wouldn't be able to find space for on a wall. My reply was that nobody in Australia had produced a calendar like this before, so we didn't know. Nevertheless, being new to publishing I was aware we had to be extremely cautious, so the answer was to print nothing before testing the market. The wildlife paintings were by brilliant wildlife artist Tony Oliver, and we produced a colour brochure with a reservation coupon allowing our readers to order it in advance.

The success of the calendar stunned everyone, including Dick. He called me at home in disbelief late one evening when he heard we had sold 10 000 copies, all through mail-order. We went on to sell over 20 000, and calendars remained our best selling Christmas present for many years.

Distribution problems

As we slowly added other products to our range the business was beginning to grow. Meanwhile, Dick had become particularly irked by the wastage involved in distributing the journal through newsagents. At that time it was sold both through newsagents and by mail direct to subscribers. Most copies went through the newsagents, in an incredible system where the distributor would, at no cost, deliver a certain number of magazines to each outlet, and at the end of that magazine's sale period the newsagents would receive credit for unsold copies by ripping their covers off and sending those back to the distributor. The magazines themselves were later picked up and pulped. This system had been going on for years, but it was extremely inefficient and environmentally wrong.

The distributor kept telling us not to worry about the wastage—that the computer would get it right after it had enough sales history to work out how many copies to send out to each newsagent. But the system never did get it right; it was a joke. Some newsagents would have far too many copies, others would have sold out quickly and be screaming for copies they couldn't get.

Dick wanted to take the journal off the stands and make it available only by subscription. By doing this we would know how many copies to print, so there would be no wastage. Also, we would have readers committed to the journal, and not be dependent on people who flicked through an issue and bought only the occasional copy. However, to take such a step would be bold, and most profit-conscious companies would not have dared go any further. We were selling up to 60 000 copies on the newsstands. What would happen if we lost most of those readers—that is, if they didn't take out subscriptions? What about the lack of visual exposure in the marketplace that would follow—would existing subscribers drop off too because the journal was not being seen anywhere? But Dick owned the company and didn't have to report to anyone. He did a lot of things for his own satisfaction, so we went ahead and in January 1988 took the journal off the newsstands.

The newsagents were livid. The journal was a popular seller and they were making money from it; their customers kept asking for it and were upset at the newsagent because they couldn't get it. Many newsagents felt we had used them as a way of getting established, then dumped them, and didn't recognise the fact that it was just too wasteful and economically stupid for an expensive journal to be distributed that way.

Our subscriptions jumped almost immediately, and climbed steadily.

Business booms

We began publishing books, including a series on regions of Australia with very detailed maps. The catalogue got larger with each issue, and we were having a lot of enjoyment. It was very different from electronics, for here we were meeting interesting adventurers, scientists, astronomers and wildlife experts. It was fascinating. Dick was now undertaking lots of flying adventures and in 1990 he was appointed chairman of the Civil Aviation Safety Authority and began spending a lot of time in Canberra.

A flyer with commercial astuteness, Dick wanted to reform the aviation regulations. He had flown himself around the world and thought Australia's regulations were forty years out of date and that he could do something to reduce the cost of flying in this country. He also wanted to make flying more affordable to get people off the roads and would say, 'Flying is 400 times safer than travelling by road. In the past twenty years 60 000 Australians have died on our roads, but not one person has been killed on a jet aircraft.' It would be a long and frustrating experience over his two-year term, attempting to influence the bureaucrats.

Meanwhile, I was having a great adventure myself, in the business. It was booming, and yet Australia in 1990 was in the middle of the worst recession experienced in our generation. The number of subscribers to the journal had grown to over 162 000 and would rise again in 1991 to 191 000. More than 80 per cent of our subscribers were renewing, an amazing result in the publishing industry. They were now scattered through sixty-five countries. The journal was running to a refined format under its key staff: founding editor, Howard Whelan; art director, Tony Gordon; cartographer, Will Pringle; and a solid team of staff writers. Dick was a hands-on editor-in-chief.

The plan to cap subscriptions

Subscribers were coming in at such a rate that in 1990 Dick considered closing off subscriptions when they reached 200 000. He said it would then be a sort of exclusive golf club where you would be put on the waiting list and when someone died, you might be able to get in! He happened to mention this one day in an interview on ABC radio, explaining, 'I'm not running *Australian Geographic* for commercial reasons. I'm running it for the satisfaction I get out of it. I sold Dick Smith Electronics because I got fed up with just sitting in an office with 500 people working for me, making lots of money but never being able to do all the wonderful things I wanted to do, and I don't want to get into the same position.' He went on to say that he was against this 'mad thing of expansion'. He said: 'I think one of the great things about Australia is our small population. Politicians are talking about growth all the time, everything's got to get bigger. In the United States you can't even drive on the freeways, you can't breathe the air, you can't even go camping without a permit because there are so many millions wanting to camp in the same area.'

In many ways I agreed with him. I had come home to Australia after leaving Dick Smith Electronics in America for these reasons too. However, whatever his listeners might have thought about that, they practically *panicked* at his suggestion that subscriptions to *Australian Geographic* might be capped. Our phones were jammed for nearly a week and they knocked out the local telephone exchange! Our subscriptions eventually peaked at about 207 000.

We dip a toe into retail

With the ever-growing list of exclusive *Australian Geographic* branded products, the mail-order business had grown from less than several hundred thousand dollars in sales in 1988 to just under three million in 1990. Our retail experience at Dick Smith Electronics gave me confidence that now we could do well if we put all our catalogue items into a shop, and Dick, despite his hesitancy at getting involved 'because he had other things to do that he had always wanted to do', agreed in October 1990 that I could go ahead with the project.

I leased a shop in a dog of a location in the city, in the same building where we had held the demonstration against Tandy sixteen years earlier, but up a flight of stairs where the rent was cheap. To run it I hired Geoff Newlyn, the young manager of a nearby outdoor/camping shop, after telling him we had signed a lease for twelve months and he might be out of a job if the experiment failed. He still took it on.

We sat down and worked out what we were going to sell based on the track history of mail-order sales, and then started buying those items along with a few of what I used to call 'wish list' products, more expensive ones that people wish they might own 'but can't afford to right now'. I wanted the ambience to be like an Australian bush experience, and we put in ingredients such as sounds of running water, bird calls and burnt oils from various native shrubs and trees to create the scents of the outdoors. Lighting was arranged to simulate shafts of sunlight penetrating the bush canopy. We made use of old corrugated iron and recycled timbers, with a colour scheme that gave an outback feel.

Some people cautioned us that it was the worst time to open a retail shop, so why not wait until the recession ended? We were concerned about the economic down-turn, but because our overheads were so low I thought even in a worst-case scenario we could at least make a small profit. On opening day, 26 March 1991, we had a full-page ad in the *Sydney Morning Herald*, announcing 'Aussie Company Busts Recession!' with a statement from Dick that said: 'We hope that opening a store will inspire all Australians in these difficult times. We have a great land, we have a great country too if we are prepared to work hard. It's time to stop whingeing and blaming others and get out and give it a go!'

We had been up all night with last-minute arrangements and the illuminated sign outside was just being installed as the doors opened to a waiting queue of customers. By the end of the first week we had made a profit. We knew that we would make it. Perhaps we could build a retail chain again? By November 1992 we had opened six Australian Geographic shops and we celebrated sales of $1 million for that month. Geoff Newlyn, who had risked losing his job if that first shop failed, went on to become general manager of our Australia-wide chain.

Recession hits but Australian Geographic booms

In 1992 our biggest worry was how we could possibly manage the sales frenzy of that Christmas period. Our warehouse, only recently purpose-built at Terrey Hills, was already out of space and hundreds of pallets had to be shipped to rented space. The company was in buzzing, delightful chaos. We were stressed, but it was a positive feeling. There was a recession, but we were booming. We were very pleased to have good jobs and to be employing more people, not retrenching them. Customers seemed almost awed by the shops and the merchandise, one writing in a shop's visitors' book, 'I am enlightened, and now know the true meaning of life!' Our subscribers wanted to buy their Christmas gifts from us, and sometimes people couldn't move in the crush and we had to hire security guards.

We were on a roll and I knew we couldn't stop. I would say to the staff, 'Look, enjoy this experience, you may never see anything like it again in your working life.' For the first six months of that financial year sales were up 314 per cent, and takings in the shops reached nearly $5 million. When I sent Dick a note to announce the result he scribbled, 'Incredible!' That December he presented a cheque for $1 million to The Smith Family Christmas Appeal.

The shopping centre owners wanted us now because we were attracting crowds to their centres, and we were able to negotiate great rent deals. At one major CBD location we were even able to strike a deal where we didn't pay rent for twelve months, including outgoings. I admit I was beginning to feel somewhat guilty that I had encouraged Dick to approve our entry into retail again, since it was the reason he had sold Dick Smith Electronics, but then I thought of all the employment we had given to local artists, craft and clothing manufacturers and other suppliers, and to the hundreds of mainly young and very bright people we employed.

Besides, the Australian Geographic Centre at Terrey Hills really was the ultimate base for fulfilling Dick's goal of giving something back to the country after his Dick Smith Electronics success. Listing his aims in the first issue of the journal, he said he wanted to keep the vital spirit of our country alive, and to help do this he wanted to give some of the proceeds from the business to fund social, environmental and adventure projects. Within the complex he had installed a Life Education Centre, where bus loads of school children arrived almost daily to be shown the dangerous effects of drugs on the human body. To get the centre started Dick had even designed and personally built some of the working models in his home workshop.

The success of the new business had enabled him to give away far more than he had anticipated, and by the end of 1991 he had donated over $5 million. We all felt a sense of achievement in this. At the centre, up to three people were employed to help manage the huge load of correspondence and phone calls that came in seeking Dick's support for this and that. In a note to our staff, Dick's secretary, Jan Dalton, gave us an insight into the great variety of daily inquiries. Among them were requests for Dick:

- to invent a tracking device to stop an autistic child escaping from home;
- to give a 24-year-old artist advice on how to promote himself;
- to become a major shareholder in an Australian company (investment of $1 million required);
- to become involved in a film;

- to give interviews about his predictions for the 1990s;
- to be aware that the lady writing had seen a policeman escorting a 10-year-old child into a police paddy wagon.

Dick wants another adventure

I knew it would be just a matter of time before both Dick and I began to lose interest and want a new challenge. Dick would be first, I thought, as I could see he had a passion to change the country's aviation regulations and to plan his latest adventure, the first crossing of Australia by balloon. He and John Wallington achieved that—the first transcontinental crossing by balloon—in 1994.

That same year Dick was the first to fly a helicopter around the world from east to west, against the prevailing winds, and he drove a solar-powered car across Australia in record-breaking time. All this created excitement throughout the business and got us lots of publicity.

While Dick was doing his ballooning and flying we were opening fourteen new retail shops—a record number for the company—to bring the chain to a total of twenty (there were eventually forty-four). But Dick had now been involved in Australian Geographic for eleven years and his interest was waning. He was seeking a new adventure, and to relieve himself of the growing financial burden and risk, in April 1995 he sold Australian Geographic Pty Ltd to John Fairfax Holdings.

Dick crosses Australia by balloon, reminding the country about Australian Geographic's 'magical shops'.

This, of course, was the same company that eight years earlier had published the report headed 'Magazine turns sour for Dick Smith'. It now paid him $41 million for it.

Chapter 5
What is it like working with Dick Smith?

People I met were fascinated to know what Dick was 'really like', and you could understand why, because something was always being reported in the media about the company and/or its founder. It appeared that the company was an exciting place to work—and so it was for most of us.

Ad man John Singleton, who got on well with Dick, once remarked to me that I must have done something wrong in a previous life to still be working with *that man*, but I did so because every year was full of excitement. There was always something unusual happening, and it was a roller-coaster ride. Hardly a day went by without a new development, an idea or a scheme being floated or implemented. Dick's restless energy for fun as an escape from business boredom was, I think, what generated the publicity that made the company stand out from the rest; the money that came in was just a sideshow to him.

He loved controversy: it seemed to give him more purpose and determination. For example, for one short period back in the early Dick Smith Electronics days some of our electronics competitors referred to the company as 'Tricky Dicky's', and a number of us weren't too happy with that, as it was untrue. Dick, however, saw it as an opportunity to get our competitors to advertise us, so put an appeal to 'Come to Tricky Dicky's' in our ads. Our rivals soon stopped using the term!

Often he would run into my office grinning like a naughty schoolboy who was about to play a prank at school. He would have an unusual plan he'd hatched the night before and he'd quickly bounce the plan off me. Sometimes we debated it, but most of the time we had a good laugh. I was more conservative and reserved than Dick when it came to taking on the multinationals, well-known personalities or the media, but more often than not he would convince me, either that it had to be done for a good cause or that it would be great fun and publicity for the business even if we lost.

Dick was very forward thinking and this helped us pick future trends in products, such as the CB radio boom and the demand for video games. He was able to sense the growing public awareness of all things Australian, which led to him launching *Australian Geographic*. Public concern about food imports and the sell-off of our icon brands to overseas interests, so that the wealth generated was repatriated to their parent companies, inspired him to start Dick Smith Foods.

Dick had a lot of enthusiastic commitment for any project he thought was worthwhile. I found it difficult not to get caught up in this energy, and when Dick was in top form he could be very, very motivating. He had a T-shirt printed that read 'Enthusiastic Amateur', and he would wear it to meetings about the need for aviation reform, one of his great interests. Those words were, in fact, used by some of his aviation industry peers as a put-down; they refused to take him seriously even though he had pioneered reform, so he wore the shirt to take the wind out of their sails.

Dick was usually optimistic, looking for the positive and not dwelling on the negative, and he was unrepentant at displaying his optimism when he set out to concentrate on the positives about Australia in the *Australian Geographic* journal. He would say that the media tended to report on what was wrong with the country, and that *Australian Geographic* would be there to focus on what was right with it and redress the balance. Some people didn't agree with this approach; even some writers who joined us left because they thought this was unbalanced reporting. Yet Dick had said right from the beginning that the journal was going to be biased towards Australia.

He wasn't an easy person to work with at times, but he was fair and never 'out to be a bastard' like some other business people I knew, who got a kick out of bullying their management or staff. People generally felt secure working with Dick because they knew they wouldn't get the sack just because he lost his temper. Dick was able to separate the person from the work they performed—it was the quality of their work that he was interested in, and the quality of the work is what he attacked if he was unhappy with it, or praised if he was pleased with it. Whichever, you knew it was genuine. We made it absolutely clear that anyone who performed could feel secure. He would say,

'Good people are hard to find and if you last more than six months here, you've got a job for life!'

People who worked for Dick could also benefit from his generosity. His loyal secretary in the early Dick Smith Electronics' days, Dawn McCallum, had an old car that was falling apart and I heard Dick ask her one day if he could borrow it to go to a meeting. She gave him the keys, apologising about the car's poor condition. When Dick returned, late, he threw the keys on her desk and quietly told

As this ad shows, we thought our 'Do Anything Dawn' McCallum was so good we once jokingly offered her for sale as one of our products!

the rest of us not to forget to look out the window when Dawn went home. Dawn left the office and we could see her going through the car park with a worried look on her face. She couldn't find her car. Finally she gave up, sure that it was stolen. It was then that Dick opened a window and yelled, 'Hey, Dawn! Check your keys and see if one fits this car over here!' He had bought her a brand new car.

Small but equally unexpected gifts of appreciation were common. *Australian Geographic* staff writer Stuart Inder, fully absorbed in editing one of Dick's adventure books, recalls Dick bouncing into his office and thrusting an expensive bottle of Scotch into his hands. 'What's this for?' Stuart asked. 'I heard you liked good whisky!' Dick shouted, already out the door. A non-drinker, Dick wouldn't know one whisky from another, but he had asked his secretary to 'go out and buy a good one'.

Dick has never been a smoker or a drinker—or a wowser. I remember him trying a cigarette at a staff picnic in the 1970s but after a few puffs and a lot of coughing he gave up. He said he couldn't see the point of it, but he was not an anti-smoker and he never complained about smoking in the workplace. In the 1980s he launched and paid for a public education campaign in the schools specifically to draw attention to the tobacco industry's targeting of youngsters, yet he never questioned the right of people to smoke.

Dick and I generally agreed on what we were trying to do operationally, and philosophically we nearly always agreed on how the business should be run. He was ruthless

Dick Smith's nightmare. How a cartoonist in the *Australian Financial Review* saw it.

in maintaining high standards, and I liked this about him because I wanted to be involved in a professional company, and at times I was tough to work with too. We got on very well, we became great friends, and although we had an occasional disagreement over a business plan or administrative issue, neither of us made it personal.

I became hardened to his occasional bluntness, took any warranted criticism constructively and kept my mind focused on the job. We knew we worked well as a combination: Dick was the shrewd marketer and public face of the company; I looked after its day-to-day management. I didn't want his job and he didn't want mine, and rarely did we cross onto each other's turf.

As a demonstration of our rapport, of his persuasive powers and his sound and simple business logic, here is the letter he handwrote to me in 1986 when I agreed to join the Australian Geographic company to work with him again:

Dear Ike,

Great to get your letter. I'm sitting in our family-room watching TV and thinking about you and me working together again. It should be great.

I see tough times ahead in Aussie however. $28 (for a subscription) should not be too much for most people to pay. Remember how our mail-orders used to be about that much on average?

Our mailing list of over 100,000 must be incredibly valuable and I can see great potential for you to sell other products, from books to T-shirts and calendars etc. We don't even have a pamphlet for new subscribers at the moment—hopeless. I am happy with expansion ideas as long as they do not cause me any extra worry. At the moment I'm quite fed-up and your acceptance has given me new enthusiasm.

I know it's a drop for you (in pay) however it's a staggering increase over what I had planned (i.e. nil position). I think you will find it an incredibly exciting job, so much potential but with so many dead losses (employees). I think you will be using your proven expertise to get good people very quickly.

I wish to spend more time adventuring and working on my social causes. I don't have the same drive for making money but still the same attitude to waste and misunderstandings. AG has the most incredible potential and it's only half way there.

By the way, there is nothing different to running DSE— exactly the same—just needs bloody good discipline and people prepared to stick to my ideas (which I've developed and copied from others).

Look forward to seeing you and Louise and kid when you all get back—I'll try and hang on until May—in the meantime it's still making a bloody fortune!

Dick's secretaries

Dick went through a few secretaries: the pressure on them was great because of the incredible number of projects he was involved in and the detailed work needed to keep track of everything. When they parted there was usually mutual agreement that it was the job, not personalities, that had caused the working relationship to fail. I haven't met one of his former secretaries who doesn't still have respect for him.

Once when we were looking for a secretary for Dick I gave this rough briefing note, listing the skills and attributes required, to the headhunters. They were horrified by the challenge!

- *Top stenographer:* Typing, shorthand, writing.
- *Meticulous at detail:* Must be phenomenal at detail, *love* attention to detail.
- *Memory:* Incredible memory for details, facts, people's names, telephone numbers, appointments.
- *A love for and knowledge of Australia:* A sound knowledge of Australia. When you're wanting to put an aircraft fuel dump at Wiluna she knows where Wiluna is.
- *Mature:* Adult-like in response to Dick's moods and lack of patience.

- *A planner:* Must be able to think ahead. 'What will Dick want?' 'What will Dick ask?' 'What will he need for a meeting?'
- *Intelligent:* Must be incredibly sharp. Maybe an honours graduate or perhaps someone who did very well at school but didn't get the chance to go to university.
- *Commonsense:* Highly intelligent, yet 'streetwise'.
- *Social skills:* Good PR vital. Someone who can make callers feel great and project enthusiasm or the way you want people to picture you (i.e. friendly, tough, compassionate).
- *Hard worker:* Prepared to put in the long hours and work without breaks where necessary, work fast, and be on call at most times.
- *Works in parallel:* Someone who can work on a multitude of tasks at one time.
- *Not interested in glamour:* Someone who doesn't expect roses on the desk, long lunches, evening business balls, flying overseas first-class with the boss.
- *Not proud*: Someone who is prepared to do anything, from filling Dick's petrol tank to getting tea and biscuits. Not a person who says or thinks 'that's not my job!'
- *Fantastic self-esteem:* When criticised does not become moody or depressed but bounces back on top. Very tough.
- *Preferably has a pilot's licence!*

And here's some practical advice on dealing with Dick from one who knows. Before Jan Dalton, one of Dick's longest serving secretaries, moved interstate, she drew up the following 'Coping With Dick Kit', with explanations for its use, and presented it to her replacement at the office farewell party. It was done without malice and with great good humour, and was one reason why Australian Geographic was a fun place to work.

- *The Helicopter Cap:* A cap with a chopper blade on the top that twirls. You wear it when Dick is away so you feel you are flying too.

- *The Set of Handcuffs:* Because Dick is so hard to pin down and his attention span is so short, you keep these in the drawer in the hope of attaching him to his desk.

- *The Compass:* Dick might be anywhere adventuring, flying or out in the bush, so the compass will let you imagine you know where he is, and inform all the people who want him urgently.

- *The Whistle:* Because nobody ever knows when Dick is returning from one of his adventures, when he appears suddenly you blow this whistle to scramble everyone.

- *The Dick Catcher:* Because Dick never keeps still and is always running off to jump into his car or his helicopter, this Dick Catcher, a butterfly net, may be handy!

- *The Magic Wand:* When the demanding boss makes a great lot of requests while asking why you hadn't done something else, you wave him away with this Magic Wand.

- *The Ultimate Solution:* This plastic toy gun in the kit is for when all else fails. Use it to put yourself out of misery!

Chapter 6
Why is Dick Smith
so successful?

Many times over the years I've been asked why Dick is so successful—as if people expected me to come out with some wondrous, instant magical formula—but if you have to find a single word, it is 'simplicity'. Dick Smith is not a complicated person, and he does not try to make himself out to be one, which is why he relates so well to other people. His unpretentiousness is one of the qualities that I appreciated more and more as I met other business leaders who radiated big egos and self-importance in all directions. The hundreds of examples of how he does business that are found in these pages demonstrate this simple, no-nonsense approach. Dick would say, 'If I can start Dick Smith Electronics and Australian Geographic, employ lots of people and make lots of dollars, it's obviously got to be very simple. I just use commonsense!'

I was in a meeting with Dick and the Woolworths people shortly after Woolworths bought a majority share in Dick Smith Electronics, and Woolworths' managing director, Tony Harding, said, 'Dick, you haven't given us a budget, but how do you think you will go in the future?'

Dick replied, 'Somewhere between making a fortune and going broke!'

The business was, in fact, making a fortune, and somebody else in Dick's position might have presented a long spiel, fully illustrated by charts, graphs and inventive financial predictions for the future, but Dick didn't know how well we were going to do in the future, so didn't make out that he did.

Dick also has an extraordinary ability to decide quickly what will and will not work, or to pick flaws in a proposal. He evaluates a plan with commonsense and logic, asking lots of questions. If sometimes he ridicules a proposal, it may be a tactic to test the presenter's own confidence in the details, or their resolve to see it through. His forward thinking has enabled him to pick trends in products before competitors.

But none of the elements in his character is unique. Most, if not all, are shared by many other successful people. Dick has been able to make his strengths work for him, and to sideline his weaknesses through a realistic self-acceptance of what he can and cannot do.

During his youth, Dick's father would tell him his problem was that he didn't have any self-discipline. Dick later agreed that his father was right. He was 24 years old when he started his car-radio business, and for the first three months there were careless mistakes and general sloppiness. Dick told me he had an inferiority complex then, for he hadn't any academic abilities, his friends had gone on to take well-paying jobs or to university and here he was lying under car dashboards trying to make a living. At this point he realised that if he continued being slack and paying no attention to detail he was going to go broke, so he started to become focused.

He disciplined himself to complete the radio job-cards fully and accurately, and to pricemark goods for sale. As he developed self-discipline he gained self-confidence, and he began to lose his feeling of inferiority and think that maybe he could make something of himself.

Here are some of the elements that helped Dick to success.

Conservative risk taking

Dick considered himself lucky that he had had a near business failure at the beginning of his career and not when the business was much larger and he could have been destroyed. That experience made him incredibly conservative—more of a risk manager—which was contrary to the public perception of him as a great risk taker. He never even invested in the share market because he said he didn't know what was going on in those companies and wasn't in control. Dick did take risks, especially on many of his adventures where he always was aware that something could go wrong, but he eliminated, or greatly reduced, the risks by meticulous planning and by using top quality equipment. We generally followed this rule in business too.

Yet Dick liked pushing himself by living on the edge and enjoyed the possibility that he could fail. He felt he was a 'tall poppy' and that the media would get him as soon as he made a slight mistake. In a strange sort of way he seemed to like this, almost as if he were playing a part in a tragic script, where in the end he would make a fateful mistake, be ruined and have to start all over again.

Hard work

We found that when it looked as if a lot of hard work and thought had gone into a project, a product or a shop, it was more commercially successful. Dick used to say, 'Customers aren't stupid. They can tell if something is lightweight.' With *Australian Geographic,* everything had to look like an amazing amount of hard work had gone into it: from the research and accuracy of the text, to the photography, maps and illustrations and the quality of the printing.

Readers can scan a magazine and tell whether hard work has gone into its production. We didn't sit around waiting for writers to send articles on spec. At *Australian Geographic* we came up with an idea for an article only after a lot of discussion, and then we commissioned a writer and photographer. The article might take twelve months to research, write and illustrate, and there would be another six months to get the illustrations and maps the way we wanted them. All this was a lot of hard work and incredibly expensive, but it was all noticeable when you looked at the finished journal.

Artist Rod Scott, who painted many of the front covers of the journal in the first few years of publication, would take months, painstakingly working on the finest detail of an animal. One day he came into my office in an exhausted state, to tell me that in the early hours of that morning he had destroyed his painting for the next issue because he was unhappy with the stance of the animal. Such was the detail and perfection that so many of our people demanded of themselves. Some magazine publishers believe text is something to fit between the advertisements, which they consider the real money-makers. We set out to do the opposite. We wanted the text to make money, and limited the amount of advertising to a few pages at the front and back.

There was almost paranoia about the importance of avoiding errors. Facts in our articles were checked by up to three independent experts before publication. We wanted the journal to be an accurate reflection of the times in which it was published. Dick used to say, 'Fifty years from now people should be able to read an AG article with the assurance that the facts in it were correct.' Some of our contributing writers, who had worked for more indulgent publishers, found this process off-putting at first, but our readers were diverse, many were very well educated and experienced, and as the journal was more expensive than any other magazine on the market, there was an expectation of quality. It made commercial sense to produce quality.

It was amazing how many letters we received when we did make an error, and we always acknowledged and corrected errors in our Postscript column, no matter how minor they were. In one article it was mentioned that a water pump had been installed in a camp in Western Australia's Kimberley region in 1986. A Melbourne reader wrote to say that the year was 1987 because he happened to be at that camp when the pump was being installed.

When the journal was first launched Dick was told by people in the publishing industry he would be lucky to get 10 000 subscribers; within a few months he had over 60 000. When eventually we had over 200 000 subscribers, we were told the journal's phenomenal success was obviously due to Dick Smith's name, but I don't doubt our initial subscribers would soon have stopped buying the journal had the writers, photographers and artists not put into each issue the hard work and attention to detail that Dick demanded.

Desire for success

Undoubtedly Dick's business successes have been helped by the fact he has never needed a lot of sleep and has a restless energy that keeps him on the go. He is able to achieve an amazing amount in a very short time. Even in conversation he has a short attention span. His lunch was, and no doubt still is, a sandwich. When he would take off from the office for hours, days or even weeks at a time on a trip or an adventure, he would have laid down enough projects, and motivated enough people with new ideas, to keep everyone occupied until he appeared again. The sound of the helicopter landing at Dick Smith Electronics, or the rollershutter rising on his garage door at Australian Geographic, gave an early announcement of his arrival back at work. There would be a scramble to hide if you hadn't completed what you were supposed to, or a mad rush to get his attention if you had. It all made great fun! Dick's energy was good for the business: it created a sense of excitement and urgency to get things done.

Dick is a keen bushwalker, and at Australian Geographic—sited, like his home, on the edge of the Ku-ring-gai National Park—we regularly awaited his arrival from his early morning bushwalk. He was so rarely sick that I suspect he was just too busy to get ill.

Dick wanted to be successful at what he did; he was acutely aware of how easy it was to fail and would often state that the difference between success and failure was a razor's edge. Perhaps this strong desire to succeed and a fear of failure have been his greatest driving force.

Yet he is not too proud to let others know of his limitations, and he has always deliberately gathered good people around him. He hires them to do the work he can't do, or doesn't do well, and often if someone on the staff becomes better at one of his tasks, he passes the responsibility to them and isn't embarrassed to say why. He doesn't mind you disagreeing with him if you have a worthwhile point of view. He never cares how old a person is, where they come from, what school they went to—they just have to do the job well. He has great difficulty sacking anyone and can persevere with them until it is hopeless to go on.

Joy from giving

Another of Dick's characteristics is that he truly gets great personal satisfaction and enjoyment from giving. I signed thousands of his cheques for charities over the years, for anything from $1000 to $1 million. More than once he has given away $1 million dollars. One Monday morning he came into my office and said he and Pip had been helping deliver Christmas hampers for The Smith Family charity at the weekend and he thought he should help their appeal with a cheque for a million, and what did I think? I agreed and was excited that we could do something so positive for the community. After he left my office I reflected on how far the business had come from the days in receivership when we had to pay cash for everything.

Pip

Dick's wife, Pip, is remarkable in her own right, and has to be included in his 'success secrets'. They became friends when she was seventeen and he twenty-two, and married two years later. They have two grown daughters they are close to. When Dick started in business at the age of twenty-two with just $610 in capital, $10 of it was Pip's. She has provided Dick with continuous support at home and enormous assistance through all his adventures and business deals. Her loyal, easy-going personality has helped her deal with Dick's occasional impulsiveness and impatience, enabling him to focus on business activities and personal fulfilment. Dick dedicated one of his many books about his adventures (*Solo Around the World*, 1992), 'To Philippa—known by everyone as Pip—without whom my personal boundaries would never have been extended. Without the patience and security she has always offered, and her willing presence and enthusiastic support in a

Dick and Pip.

hundred and one unlikely places around the globe, my adventures would be less fulfilling, and some might never have taken place.'

Honesty

Dick's honesty and forthrightness made it easier for me to work with him, because he had no hidden agenda. He once proposed publicly that Australia would be better served if the Taxation Office ceased publishing its annual list of those it fined for evading taxes and replaced it with a list of people who paid the most tax, 'because there would be great rivalry to be on it'.

Dick would say the way to be successful was to be absolutely honest, that your dishonesty would be used against you in some later situation. I saw him proved right. One day an employee of our purchasing section came to Dick and me and, believing that he would impress us, said that we had received from Hong Kong some metal amplifier cases with transformers packed inside them to maximise use of space, and the transformers had, as a result, cleared customs without us having to pay duty on them.

Dick immediately said the man would have to go and pay the duty. The employee said he thought that was stupid, because no one knew about it. Dick said, 'Well, I know about it, and it is a business principle that customs be paid. If people find me conning the Customs Department, they are obviously going to con me.' The duty was paid.

Some time later we caught the same employee in some dishonest dealings and took him to court. While Dick was discussing aspects of the case with counsel, the barrister asked Dick if his 'hands were clean'. He said, 'You're a businessman and he must have something on you. You can depend on him to get up in court and say what you've done wrong.' Dick had done nothing wrong and the employee made no allegations, but can you imagine the headlines if they had been able to ask Dick if it were true

Dick used his own resources to take on the cigarette companies with hard-hitting ads like this.

he had evaded duty on a shipment of transformers, and he had had to answer yes?

Dick is very direct in his dealings with people, which sometimes got him into trouble with the super-sensitive. He was not frightened to take on government authorities, or powerful individuals and industries, if he thought it necessary. He was fortunate to be in a position where he could say what the public actually felt about an issue, while most politicians or business leaders wouldn't. He could, for example, get up and defend Australian businesses in a way many other business leaders couldn't because their businesses were owned overseas and so they needed to be cautious about what they said; but he could also be critical of business, whereas many politicians were unprepared to get big business off-side.

He took on the powerful cigarette companies when he felt the work and the money he was putting into Life Education, the drug educational program, was being undermined by slick advertising aimed at exploiting young people. As he put it, they were capitalists who were lying, who should have come out and honestly said, 'Yes, we are exploiting kids—that's our market. It's a legal product and we need to recruit more people to buy it.' He once said to me that his father fought in World War II for freedom and, in his honour, he was not going to be gutless but would stand up for principles he felt were important for the country.

Scepticism

I suspect Dick was born a sceptic, and I have no doubt this has served him well in business. I learned this very early when I saw outsiders present ideas or deals for the business and he would see any flaw in a proposal almost immediately. He was quickly able to spot charlatans, challenging them with a number of reasons why something couldn't be true, or why their plan wouldn't work. He was a subscriber to the American sceptic publication *The Zetetic,* became a member of the United States-based Committee for the Scientific Investigation of Claims of the Paranormal and later became patron of Australian Sceptics.

Yet I am sure Dick had an open mind about the existence of the paranormal. He simply couldn't believe in astrology, numerology, flying saucers, clairvoyance, the Bermuda Triangle, pyramid energy, ESP, psychic healing, water divining or the claim that Uri Geller used paranormal powers to bend spoons. It upset him that sick people would, in desperation, pay money to be 'cured' by fake healers.

I recall that in the 1970s, when there was a lot of media interest in Erich Von Daniken and Nostradamus, he would laugh and ask, 'How can anyone believe such absolute rubbish!' So, he mounted a $100 000 challenge in a science magazine, announcing:

> I will give $100 000 to anyone who can show me that they can water-divine or that they have paranormal power. The conditions are perfectly straight forward. The main one is that we agree to set up a simple test, one that you recognise and any reasonable person would recognise, as being a fair test. It also has to be something that the scientific community will accept. Simply to save time, I ask that anyone who wishes to take up the challenge writes to me first so that a preliminary test can be done. This would involve demonstrating their ability before an impartial observer, such as a schoolteacher or local librarian.

The cynics told me Dick would never pay out the money, that he would find a way of getting around it; that it was just a promotional stunt. They were absolutely wrong. Dick would have been *ecstatic* at having to pay out the reward if the existence of the paranormal was proved. He would have considered his hundred grand well spent in return for the millions in publicity he would have got for being the person to show that the paranormal exists. Needless to say, he had no claimants.

However, in 1980 he brought the Canadian magician James Randi to Australia to help conduct a series of divining tests for water and gold. The prize money was $40 000 for a successful demonstration by one of the participants. Dick arranged for the demonstration to take place in a vacant paddock near our Dick Smith Electronics North Ryde office, which he had levelled. He buried, a few centimetres below ground, ten 100 mm plastic pipes in a grid pattern. Valves had been installed on the pipes so that any one of them could be opened to allow the water to flow through on a judge's signal. The late Reverend Ted Noffs was there as an official witness. Sixteen contestants signed up for the test, about half choosing to divine for water and the others for a $22 000 gold ingot Dick had borrowed from a bank and buried in a box. The diviners chose to use a variety of devices, including L-shaped metal rods, forked sticks and pendulums.

The success rate for divining accurately was *abysmal*.

Dick felt quite badly about this because he thought the public exposure would have a devastating effect on the diviners. James told Dick not to worry, that the diviners would still believe they could divine. He was right: the diviners claimed it was the test that was flawed! One explanation put forward was that it didn't work because of the money incentive (greed); another was that there was high sunspot activity that day, which hampered their ability; and others were that magnets were buried in the ground or that there was interference from portable radio transmitters in the area.

James Randi's theory was that the diviners got such wild reactions from their various types of apparatus not from paranormal ability but from a state of mind, known as the 'ideomotor effect', where the brain *unconsciously* initiates movement towards the point where the diviner believes the object is located. As proof, he arranged a demonstration in Dick's office with a reporter present. He asked Dick to get an audio speaker from the warehouse, and he put it in a cardboard box after showing the reporter how the magnet on the speaker would attract a bent piece of metal wire brought near it. He then handed the reporter the wire. The reporter walked towards the box, and was amazed as the wire sharply swung towards it each time he passed near it.

James then opened up the box and lifted the speaker out, revealing that he had secretly removed the magnet from it. The reporter was stunned, but even more so to find that now that he knew the magnet was missing, he couldn't get the wire to move towards the speaker.

Several weeks later, James Randi went on Channel 9's *Don Lane Show* and started to challenge the psychic abilities of Mrs Doris Stokes, who was a favourite regular guest on the show. Don Lane became furious, stood up, swept a heap of broken spoons and bent keys from the table in front of them and stormed off the set, leaving James sitting there in front of the cameras. Don Lane's uncharacteristic anger created an enormous and unexpected amount of publicity, which wasn't bad for Dick Smith Electronics.

Unfortunately, for many years we would continue to receive phone calls and letters from people describing their paranormal capabilities, and Dick became frustrated at having to spend so much time dealing with them. He had a rubber stamp made that read, 'SEE YOUR DOCTOR!' and planned to stamp it on letters from the wackiest of his 'raving lunatics' and return them to the senders.

Dick never dared to use it, but Garry Crapp, our National Service Manager, did on some of the weirder technical proposals and claims he received!

Love of adventure

Dick would say to me that adventure was his 'drug' and he considered Dick Smith Electronics—not flying a helicopter solo around the world, ballooning across Australia or landing at the North Pole—to be his greatest adventure. To Dick an adventure was something he had never done before: it had to have an unpredictable outcome, involve risk and have a chance of success.

Dick Smith Electronics met that criteria: when he started he had $610, he was young and naïve in business, and he didn't know where it would all end up. But as with his other adventures, when it was over and he had sold the business, he had no regrets—he moved on to the next adventure. There is just not the space to list here, let alone detail, all his various adventures on land, water and air. Accounts of his aviation exploits fill several books, from *The Earth Beneath Me* (1983), to *Our Fantastic Planet* (1991), *Solo Around the World* (1992) and *Above the World* (1996).

Dick's first significant adventure was in 1964 when, at twenty, he was part of an expedition to climb Ball's Pyramid off Lord Howe Island—they didn't make it then, but fifteen years later Dick climbed it successfully. At the age of twenty-two in 1966, as a Rover Scout, he went climbing in Switzerland. (Sixteen years later, he happened to retrace part of his climb route while flying his own helicopter round the world.) He got his pilot's licence in 1973 and bought his first plane, a Twin Comanche, in 1975. In 1979 he learned to fly helicopters and bought his first, a single-engine Bell JetRanger. He flew it to Lord Howe Island and on camping trips all round Australia.

In 1982–83 it was in a later model JetRanger, registered as DIK, that Dick made his 61 000 km solo flight around the world, beginning and ending in Fort Worth, Texas. The fact that he made the flight in three stages—Fort Worth–London (across the Atlantic), London–Sydney and Sydney–Fort Worth (across the North Pacific)—meant that we saw him back in the office between stages, and he kept in regular touch with the business while he was away anyway. And, of course, his travels were always in the news. His flight was the first time a helicopter had been flown solo around the world and proved, as Dick expected, that

Dallas Times Herald

SATURDAY, JULY 23, 1983   25 Cents

WELCOME BACK DICK
"FIRST HELICOPTER ... ND THE WORLD"

— Photo by Ed Seckell

Dick Smith said he wanted to prove that he could make the trip alone and without a large support group

Whirlwind tour
Australian ends globe-circling helicopter flight of fancy

The Dallas papers welcomed Dick back from his around-the-world solo flight.

the helicopter, even single-engined, had to be considered a reliable long-distance machine.

Dick says he is a loner at heart, and so he also chose to fly solo on his three attempts to reach the North Pole by helicopter. His first was in April 1986, when he got within 648 km of the Pole. He made his second attempt that July and was within 165 km of the Pole before turning back. In each attempt the cold and the weather defeated both him and the machine because he flew without a heater to save on fuel. The following April he successfully reached the Pole after having fitted a heater and ferried fuel out onto the ice to overcome the fuel constraints.

Dick's 85 458 km flight longitudinally around the world landing at both Poles in 1988–89 was in a Twin Otter fixed-wing aircraft, and it was also the first time that had been done. With co-pilots, he made the journey in three stages between November 1988 and May 1989, the seasons influencing the flight plan. Summer at the South Pole meant winter (and inadequate light) at the North Pole. His flight began in Sydney and took him to the South Pole, on over Antarctica to Punta Arenas, Chile, north through the American continents and to the North Pole, and south again to Sydney through the Soviet Union, China and South-East Asia. Dick was the first private flyer to be given authority by the Soviet Union to pass through the centre of Siberia and Mongolia, which was the most practical route. Friendly Soviet airport staff expressed amazement that Dick personally owned the aircraft he was flying, and he got a laugh when he explained he could do it because he was a capitalist! Dick spent 336 hours in the air, but again we saw Dick between stages, as active as ever in the business. His adventures seemed to give him even more energy.

In June 1993 Australian Geographic staff were involved in the excitement of supporting Dick and John Wallington when they made the first successful flight in a balloon, *Australian Geographic Flyer*, across Australia from west to east (3867 km in 40 hours 20 minutes).

In February 2000 Dick and John set another balloon record by crossing the Tasman from east to west from Kaitaia, northern New Zealand, to the New South Wales north coast in 55 hours 17 minutes, the first Tasman crossing by balloon. The flight promoted Dick's new company, Dick Smith Foods.

Meanwhile, Dick had been involved in solar car drives across Australia from north to south and from the west coast to the east coast, and he had made another helicopter flight around the world, this time the first from east to west against the prevailing winds.

And yet, this is only a selection of the exploits of Dick Smith, Adventurer. Many of his major adventures not only recovered their costs, but actually made a profit through commercial endorsements, books and films, and that doesn't take account of the publicity Dick's companies got through his name.

Dick at the North Magnetic Pole. He finally reaches the North Pole by helicopter in 1987 on his third attempt.

Success the Dick Smith Way: Career highlights

6 August 1968

Dick Smith Electronics business opens at the Big Bear, Neutral Bay, Sydney, selling and installing car radios and two-way transceivers. Rent $15 p.w.

February 1969

Dick Smith relocates the car radio business to get high profile road exposure at 162 Pacific Highway, Gore Hill. Rent $120 p.w. Sales are approximately $64 000 for the financial year.

July 1969

First 'Dick Smith Car Radio Nut' advertisement.

1 July 1971

Dick Smith Wholesale, a new business selling electronic components and accessories, opens to the public at Atchison Street, St Leonards.

22 November 1971

Dick Smith Wholesale goes into receivership owing $18 000 to creditors.

July 1972

First catalogue is produced. Aimed at the electronics enthusiast and priced at 50 cents, it includes useful reference data and becomes one of the best sellers in the shop.

October 1972

Ike Bain, then 20 years old, joins the company as a service technician repairing two-way radios.

December 1972

The Dick Smith Wholesale shop at Atchison Street, St Leonards moves to 160 Pacific Highway, Gore Hill, next door to the car-radio business. Total sales for the financial year are approximately $400 000.

March 1973

Ike Bain convinces Dick Smith to let him have a go managing the shop for a trial period. Within a few weeks he is appointed manager.

October 1973

The first shop is now out of receivership. The car-radio business is sold.

June 1974

The enlarged shop at Gore Hill, with its self-serve concept, booms beyond all expectations so another shop is opened, on the Hume Highway at Bankstown.

July 1974

Dick Smith gets his first free publicity with his petrol-powered pogo stick.

May 1975

The first city store opens at York Street in Sydney. A few months later the American chain Tandy Electronics opens just a few metres away to compete head on.

June 1975

Ike Bain is appointed general manager. Sales for the financial year are $2.3 million, from three stores.

October 1975

Dick Smith Electronics management and staff demonstrate against American-owned Tandy Electronics.

April 1976

First interstate store opens in Melbourne, followed by one in Brisbane. Total number of stores is now five.

June 1976

Boom in CB radio begins. Sales reach $4.1 million.

July 1976

Dick Smith installs the NO sign in his office.

13 February 1977

First charter of Qantas Boeing 747 to the South Magnetic Pole. Eight stores are now open and sales ending June 1977 total $7.35 million, with 104 employees.

Success the Dick Smith Way: Career highlights (*cont'd*)

June 1977

CB radio is legalised.

18 September 1977

Lasseter's Gold Reef Expedition Qantas flight to locate the fabled reef.

December 1977

CB radio boom ends; many companies collapse.

March 1978

A world record for a car on water is set by Dick and adventurer Hans Tholstrup.

1 April 1978

April Fool's iceberg towed into Sydney Harbour, generating world publicity.

20 June 1978

Winchcombe Carson makes takeover offer of $6 million for Dick Smith's companies.

Dick and Ike with host Roger Climpson after the 1978 *This is Your Life* television show.

18 August 1978

Dick Smith is surprised with television show *This is Your Life*, hosted by Roger Climpson. Later that month he finds early aviator Keith Anderson's ill-fated *Kookaburra* aircraft, which had been lost for nearly fifty years.

January 1979

Work begins on new head office and distribution centre at North Ryde. Dick Smith takes delivery of a Bell JetRanger helicopter and obtains his helicopter licence the following month.

March 1979

Dick Smith Electronics opens an office and retail outlet in Hong Kong but closes the following year. There are now twelve stores trading.

June 1979

Sales for the financial year reach $13.1 million, with 186 employees.

29 August 1980

Dick sells 60 per cent of Dick Smith Electronics chain of seventeen stores, with a turnover of $17 million, to Woolworths. Net profit before tax is $3.5 million, with 245 employees.

30 August 1980

Dick Smith and adventurer Hans Tholstrup jump over seventeen motorbikes in a double-decker bus.

14 September 1980

Boeing 747 flight of Smith passengers raises money for the Smith Family charity. Everyone, including the crew, are Smiths.

October 1980

Ike Bain is appointed managing director of Dick Smith Electronics.

March 1981

Dick Smith Electronics opens in Auckland, New Zealand.

Success the Dick Smith Way: Career highlights (*cont'd*)

30 June 1982

Dick sells remaining 40 per cent of Dick Smith Electronics to Woolworths. Sales for the year total $32.2 million from thirty-three stores, with 393 employees.

5 August 1982

Dick Smith commences his solo helicopter flight around the world from Fort Worth, Texas.

22 July 1983

Dick Smith arrives at Fort Worth, Texas, completing the first solo flight by helicopter around the world.

30 June 1984

Dick Smith Electronics opens its fiftieth retail store in Australia. Sales are $46.6 million, with over 500 employees.

July 1984

Dick begins work on new journal to be called *Australian Geographic*.

January 1985

Dick Smith Electronics Inc. is established in Redwood City, California and Ike Bain relocates there for two years. First retail store opens in April that year.

June 1985

First Bourke to Burketown Bash.

January 1986

First issue of *Australian Geographic* launched.

15 April 1986

Dick Smith makes first attempt to fly solo to the North Pole by helicopter; he nearly dies in cold and vertigo attack.

28 July 1986

On second attempt, Dick Smith gets within 165 km of the Pole.

January 1987

Dick Smith is named Australian of the Year. 'Couple In the Wilderness' experiment is announced.

29 April 1987

Dick Smith, on third attempt, lands at the North Pole.

May 1987

Ike Bain is appointed CEO of Australian Geographic Pty Ltd.

1 November 1988

Dick Smith and Giles Kershaw depart Sydney in a Twin-Otter on the first flight to circle the world via both Poles. The 85 000 km journey was completed on 28 May 1989.

26 March 1991

First retail Australian Geographic shop opens as an experiment next door to Dick Smith Electronics in York Street, Sydney. The new concept is an immediate success and is followed by another shop, at Chatswood. December sales that year for the two small shops reach $500 000.

Captain Dick Smith is farewelled on his round-the-world solo helicopter flight by Ike and (from left) Ike's wife, Louise, Pip Smith and secretary Dawn McCallum with Hayley Smith.

Success the Dick Smith Way: Career highlights (*cont'd*)

1992–1994

Rapid expansion of the business takes place. During this time there are a record 207 000 subscribers to *Australian Geographic* journal and twenty-five retail stores are open and trading.

21 February 1994

Dick Smith commences first helicopter flight around the world from east to west; completes flight June 1995.

April 1995

Australian Geographic Pty Ltd and its Australian Geographic shops are sold to John Fairfax Holdings. Dick Smith remains chairman of the Australian Geographic Society and Ike Bain remains CEO of the business.

December 1997

Ike Bain resigns as Australian Geographic CEO to pursue his own business interests. He continues his association with Dick Smith as an adviser on his management committee.

December 1998

John Fairfax Holdings sells Australian Geographic to a management buyout syndicate.

January 2000

Dick Smith starts a new business, Dick Smith Foods, selling and promoting Australian produce.

Part 2
THE DICK SMITH WAY

Chapter 7
On sales and marketing

Give your business a personality

Many attributes made Dick a successful businessman, but it is his personality that for years has attracted the public. Dick Smith gave Dick Smith Electronics and Australian Geographic his personality. His name and the logo of his bright, smiling face became instantly recognisable and I found that people were happier doing business with something more than a faceless, impersonal, company structure. There is a lesson there. If you are starting a business, consider giving it your own name.

We had our electronics stores painted out with the 'Dickhead' logo, as we called it within the business. All our advertising was written in 'Dickspeak'—pitched at Dick's level of no-nonsense vocabulary—and read as though Dick was speaking to the buyer directly.

We used a lot of humour in our ads. It was fun, and often quite hilarious, planning and writing them. Dick and the team would get together and, amid howls of laughter, try to outdo each other with a more bizarre idea for marketing copy. At the time we had a brilliant copywriter, Ross Tester, an artist-designer, Mike Middleton, and a string of marketeers, such as Gary Johnston, all of them having a wicked sense of humour. The Dick Smith catalogues became sought after for their entertainment value.

As Dick's business interests changed, as they did because of the community and environmental issues that concerned Australian Geographic, so did his business image and our advertising. So successful was the personality marketing for Dick Smith Electronics and Australian Geographic that many customers believed Dick did everything and was responsible for everything, including anything that got stuffed up—so a word of warning here! If you are going to market the head of your company there will be an obligation on that person to act responsibly. Fortunately for us, we never had to worry about Dick being embroiled in a scandal. Dick Smith's good name has been a huge asset in his businesses.

Do things that get your business free media coverage

The media are always looking for something entertaining, or a personality who is stimulating, so if you can come up with a good idea they may cover it for nothing. Our business was built up on a dearth of money for advertising, but we gave value to the media and got publicity in return. Dick was a genius at getting publicity, but he also enjoyed the fun, and so did the staff, which was great for morale. In this book you'll come across mention of his more memorable public performances. While you're smiling, don't forget the message. Free publicity!

Be different from your competitors

My earliest celebration of the marketing value of difference was when the first imported electronics shipment arrived at our small Gore Hill store. We had ordered two models of a power-supply unit and asked the Chinese manufacturers to brand them with our company name. When we opened the first box, to our horror the name on the model read, 'Little Dick' power supply! But there were peals of laughter, soon almost uncontrollable, when we opened up the second model, which was branded 'Big Dick' power supply. Now, most companies would have returned them, but we saw a marketing opportunity and put them on sale. The more powerful Big Dick sold for twice the price of the Little Dick, but few asked for 'a Little Dick'. Sales of Big Dicks were huge—and we made a small fortune! Being different—being entertaining or controversial—helps people remember your business rather than somebody else's.

Go the catalogue way

One of the vital ingredients in our successful business formula was the catalogue we produced every year. It was a highly efficient way of communicating, for it led the way into people's homes long before we opened stores close to them. The result was that we had a loyal following of catalogue shoppers who immediately came into the stores in droves when we did open in their area. There was a sort of 'open day frenzy', as wide-eyed catalogue shoppers confronted all our merchandise 'live' and embarked on a spending spree. They would bring with them a list of everything they wanted from the catalogue, and then add to it.

The catalogue was sought after because it didn't contain just the range of gadgets and gizmos we sold, it had many pages of useful data that hobbyists could refer to in working on their own projects or hobbies—so it could be found on their workbenches throughout the year. We also included information about the company, our achievements, our future plans and the challenges we faced. We even put a price on the catalogue, which customers recouped with redeemable coupons against their next purchase. Our hobbyists felt they were sharing the adventure with us. Many literally were, because we put in notices asking for more hobbyists to come and join our sales staff!

We wrote the catalogue in a conversational style that appealed to our readers and, as hobbyists ourselves, we would often include some fun 'inventions', such as our Co-Tanger car aerial and 'energy saving' light globes.

The catalogue was not only a silent salesperson selling product to its readers. it was a great sales training tool for our staff. It had a lot of information and technical specifications, and the product's description included features and benefits, all of which helped them to sell by adding to their knowledge.

At Australian Geographic we used the same proven success formula to pioneer the business. Again, we tailored the product range to the interests of the journal's readers—bushwalkers, adventurers, bird-watchers, travellers and keen followers of nature. The Australian Geographic catalogue

★ CO-TANGER CAR AERIAL ★

Had your car aerial ripped off, bent over, stolen or otherwise vandalized?

Here's the answer! **FIRST TIME IN AMERICA!**

This shape has proven to be very popular but you can easily alter it to suit your area, station or personal taste.

Developed and produced in Australia after an incredible amount of complex and expensive research – the CO-TANGER AERIAL. As used by thousands of Australian car owners. Early models were based fairly closely on the old Word War II Radio Direction Finding Loops (RDF) which are still found on DC-3's and Beech 18's. However, through years of development and individual experimentation, models are available which can be fine tuned to give you fantastic performance in your own area. The co-tanger can even be modified to suit the styling of your automobile or your own aesthetic tastes.

Just look at these features:

- Suits any type, make, model or year of automobile or truck.
- Tuneable to any radio station for peak listening performance.
- Shape may be varied to suit your tastes or your car styling.
- Bending through vandalisation may even improve performance.
- No one would be stupid enough to steal it.
- We do not claim that it will increase the resale value of your auto.

Cut here and insert into broken aerial base.

Cat A-9999

FAIR DINKUM VALUE AT $395.00

(or you can make your own from a spare coat hanger for nothing)

The really amazing Co-Tanger car aerial, the fantastic energy-saving light bulb and the technologically advanced fuse!

ENERGY SAVING LIGHT BULBS

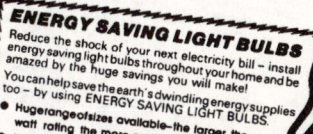

Reduce the shock of your next electricity bill – install energy saving light bulbs throughout your home and be amazed by the huge savings you will make!

You can help save the earth's dwindling energy supplies too – by using ENERGY SAVING LIGHT BULBS.

- Huge range of sizes available–the larger the watt rating the more energy you save.
- Pre-blown to save your time
- Guaranteed never to use electrical energy.

		Sizes and Savings
Cat S-9999	60 watt	$49.50 Proven Saver
Cat S-9991	80 watt	$69.50 You'll notice the savings as soon as you turn it on.
Cat S-9992	100 watt	$79.50 Most popular saver
Cat S-9993	200 watt	$89.50 A real savings boost. You'll save this cost over and over
Cat S-9994	400 watt	$99.50 The big bucks saver

Just think! For less than $100 you can save 400 watt hours every hour.

You may not believe these savings so we suggest you try any pre-blown light bulb you have in the house for your next billing period to test the results.

Giant Handbook of Electrical Circuits

Raymond A Collins–880 pages
Giant isn't the word: its a whopping 880 pages! With 60 chapters covering everything from crystal sets to computer circuitry, you're sure to find what you want here!

Cat B-1780 **$19.95**
Opening Special $14.95

Fuses & AC Products

Amazing Technological Breakthrough!

Dick Smith introduces the
NAILER 6°

A quantum leap in technology that instantly replaces any fuse wherever the amperage! Why confuse yourself with loose fuses whose ratings you've forgotten.

for only **$999**

Put this in your tool box or kitchen drawer today!

HOW THINGS WORK VOLUME 2 OUT NOW $5.95!

Another 600 pages of easily understood explanations of machines. Volume 1 has been a sell out. Now Volume 2 tells you about a whole lot more — how colour TV is transmitted, why is dry cleaning called dry, how does a computer compute. Ideal for the layman and anyone with inquisitive kids. Covers the simplest household gadget through to radar and jet engines.

We have special stocks of both volume 1 and 2 at **$5.95** each or get the pair for **$11.50** (P & P $1.10 per volume $1.50 pair).

Reference Data for Radio Engineers

(1196 pages). This massive book contains everything you need to know. Over 1½ million copies sold all over the world. Contributions from 100 leaders-in-their-fields, engineers, professors, government experts and staff of ITT. 45 chapters, 100s of charts, nomographs, diagrams, curves, tables, pictures. Yes there's 1196 pages full of everything. We have a large quantity of the latest edition still at **$26.50** post FREE. Postage is normally over $2.00 because it's so heavy!

FANTASTIC TAPE SPECIAL Genuine BASF LH SM tape in C90's. Nothing but the best do not confuse with cheaper rainbow pack. Guaranteed low noise special mechanics non-jam tape. Orders may be assorted. C90SM normal list price $3.99. Our special price 10 off **$2.20**, 20 off **$2.00**. C90SM (CrO2) Chromes normally $5.60. 10 off **$2.75**, 20 off **$2.50**. P & P $1.50 for 10, $2.50 for 20.

NEW ARRL HANDBOOK IN Latest edition has more Tx and Rx circuits than ever before plus half-size 20M Yagi and 5 element cubical quad. New updated chapters on many subjects. First shipment due end of January at $7.50 (P & P $1.00).

FRE WIT O

Chassis Hole Punch Kit Saves you a dollar. Normally $9.50 now only **$8.50** (P & P $1.00).

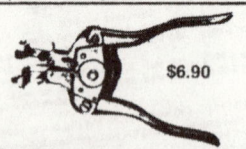

$6.90

J 5080 Wire stripper. The deluxe automatic stripper that handles all wires up to 5/16" insulation diameter. Fitted with stop for production use. In catalogue at $9.65. Save over $2.50 at only **$6.90** (P & P 75c).

J4735 Driver Kit A handy 6 piece jewellers set with free turning barrels in see through vinyl case. Usually $1.85 cut to **$1.40** (P & P 50c).

$3.50

...ond Scriber

...n from the USA — looks just like a ...int but has diamond in the nib. 6" ...astic handle. Ideal for marking PCBs ...talwork. Excellent too for cutting ...d tiles etc. Small size is ideal for ...d spaces. Manufacturer claims they ...d to cut IC chips!

Lenk Cordless Iron

The BP100 is the greatest development yet. Runs off a rechargeable cell giving up to 120 joints per charge. Press the button for soldering heat in only 5 seconds plus built-in working light.

Ideal for use on cars, caravans, boats etc. Anywhere you can't trail mains leads. Serviceman's dream. Ideal for CMOS and delicate IC circuits since there are no earth leakage currents. Only for electronic soldering (won't mend kettles!). Iron complete with tip at only **$19.95**. Mains charger BP100AC only $10 or build a 6V or 12V car charger for only 50 cents (P & P $1.00) 90 day guarantee. Spares available.

$1.40

SPECIAL MAGNIFYING GLASS for readers of Dick Smith adverts. 3" diameter. DOESN'T ENLARGE PRICES!! ONLY 95c

Our catalogues, like many of our full-page ads, were so packed with great information in small type that a magnifying glass was needed to read them. Nobody seemed to complain—and, anyway, we sold magnifying glasses!

became so popular for its new and unusual gift ideas that naturally we had calls from people asking how they could get a copy. When we replied that it was inserted in every issue of the journal and that only journal subscribers could get it, many would take out a subscription to get the catalogue! (As the catalogue got fatter, the in-house joke among the editorial writers was, 'When do we start inserting the journal into the catalogue?')

Don't discount

I don't believe in discount sales. 'You can only con a customer once', I'd say to our staff. The day we opened our first Australian Geographic shop a woman came up to me and asked, 'How much is that wind chime?' I said, '$129', and she asked, 'When is your sale?' I paused for a few seconds and announced, 'We don't have sales', and she said, 'Okay, I'll take it now!' I decided we wouldn't ever have a full-blown sale, and especially the kind of massive discounts that retailers now have in January. Too many retailers think the public is gullible. They expect them to pay full price for a few weeks leading to Christmas, then demonstrate to them a week or two later that they paid too much.

This is one reason why January retail turnover is growing every year, as people hold back their pre-Christmas spending. And gift certificates are growing in popularity, because if you give your friends certificates for Christmas they can buy up to twice as much in January.

At Australian Geographic we never discounted a subscription. We gave no discount for a two-year subscription or longer, and we were probably the most expensive magazine on the market. We gave away no bars of gold, cars or other gifts to entice customers to subscribe. We wanted loyal subscribers who were interested in the product, not in a free offer. Our subscription renewal rate was the highest in the publishing industry.

Anyone can give something away; it's lazy marketing that can take your product down market. What you have to do is focus on making your product unique and of such quality and value that it sells itself.

Don't forget the customer

Recently large hardware and office supply stores opened near where I live. I shopped at both, wandering around the huge complexes marvelling at the enormous ranges to select from. I was impressed by the effort, professionalism and expense that both companies had gone to with their newly constructed buildings, customer parking and shop fitouts. I didn't mind not being able to find anyone to serve me among the many aisles of merchandise, but what I did get agitated about was trying to get someone to take my money. Both of these huge stores had only one person at the checkout. I've been back several times since and the same thing has happened, or I have waited in a queue of customers while a lone cashier sends out a frantic, unanswered plea on the PA for a price on an item that hasn't got a barcode. It's unbelievable how both these companies have spent millions of dollars investing in plant and equipment in these shops and have forgotten to look after the customer, the source of their profits, by investing in enough people to provide customer service. They have done so much so well, but failed in something so simple.

Know what your competitors are up to

You have to shop at your competitors' stores; call them up to see what their telephone service is like; visit their web sites; place orders with them; and talk to their disgruntled staff when they apply for a job with you. Before we launched any new major product we checked the market to see what product we'd be up against. Sometimes we held off because our product wasn't competitive and added a feature to it that made it unique, or different.

Occasionally over the years our efforts at keeping an eye on our competitors backfired, as happened when I asked our mail-order manager to place an order with Altronics, a company that had a mail-order catalogue in electronics. He was to make some technical queries to discover if, and how, they answered them. I told our manager to use his home address and I would reimburse him for anything he bought. I assumed, but I shouldn't have, that he would mail the order in his local postal box, and was unaware that he put it through the office franking machine. The envelope went out with a huge postage sticker with our 'Dickhead' trademark on it! Several days later I received a call from Altronics' owner, Jack O'Donnel, whom I knew well. 'Hi, Ike!' said Jack. 'I've just got your order, I've personally answered the queries and the stuff is being despatched today. Tell me what you think of our service!'

Then there was the time we sent one of our staff to sit in his car outside a competitor's shop to survey the traffic going in and out and note how many people left with a shopping bag. He was there for some hours when there was a tap at his car window and this burly police officer demanded to know what he was doing. The shop manager had called the police, suspecting that the shop was being set up for a robbery, and our cover was blown!

Apart from competitive pricing, we also wanted to be competitive on employee pay and benefits, so one of our staff volunteered to sit for a job interview with our competitor, Tandy Electronics. (We assured him that if the job was better than ours, he was free to take it!) At Tandy's head office he was sitting in the reception area when the receptionist suggested he have something to read and handed him their staff magazine. The first thing he saw was a picture of himself on our trade stand, one of a number of pictures of trade exhibits at a recent computer show at which Tandy had also exhibited. He was so unnerved that he panicked and ran from the building, clutching the magazine. We all had a great laugh when he returned to our office, still shaken at what he considered to be a narrow escape.

Answer telephones, answer correspondence

While in a shop recently I heard a plea from the receptionist over the PA for anyone in sales to answer a customer's phone query. I could hear each section of the shop being paged, and each time there would be an unhelpful, uninterested response of, 'no, not me', 'no, I can't'. Their manner and tone indicated that they really couldn't care less. It is difficult to believe that anyone in a business that deals with the public would condone this, but it happens too often, and usually because the employees are reflecting the owner's or manager's own attitude. At Dick Smith Electronics, Dick often used to say that if he started a business again he could make it a success no matter how competitive the industry, simply by offering better customer service. We weren't perfect but we aimed to answer all correspondence. To speed it up we often used to rubber stamp the customer's original letter with the following: 'We apologise for the informal manner of this reply, but a speedy reply is better than no reply!' We then answered the customer's questions by handwriting the answers next to them, and posted back their letter. I never got a complaint about this, for the customer got a quick answer.

Take complaints seriously

I put up a notice at every sales counter in each of our Dick Smith stores, and in our catalogue, that said, 'If you have any complaints, call or write to our Managing Director, Ike Bain'. I added a phone number and address. All the staff knew I took complaints seriously: I would accept the occasional genuine mistake, but I wouldn't tolerate rudeness to customers. Other business people I knew told me I must be crazy to want to talk to complaining customers, but the surprising thing is that I very rarely got calls or letters as a result of these signs. Even today I don't know whether that's because (a) the staff rarely offended anyone, (b) an offended customer felt sorry for the employee in case he or she got the sack, (c) the staff resolved the complaint satisfactorily before it got to me, or (d) few people took the signs seriously! One complaint I did get was very late at night from a customer who found my home address in the phone book and phoned me from a box in the next street after getting lost. He had a faulty power unit with him and wanted me to replace it. When I told him I didn't keep stock at home, he proposed that he follow me to the warehouse so I could get him a new one. That's business! Occasionally I was able to handle phone complaints by telling the caller I was transferring them to our service manager, 'whose name', I announced, 'is Crapp!' I didn't hear another squeak from them before I transferred them to Garry Crapp who, of course, gave them full attention.

Service, service, service

In my talks with our sales staff I would include the example of the two petrol stations in the area where I regularly bought my petrol. They were located side by side and usually sold fuel at the same price, but one of them gave better service. Most of the staff at that station greeted customers by their first names, they made us feel they were appreciative of our business, and when I was in a queue waiting to be served they acknowledged my presence and apologised for keeping me waiting. I saw them treating other customers the same way, whether or not they knew their names. Who would you spend your money with? To care about your customers is an incredibly simple thing to do, yet only the good retailers do it.

Recently I was in a restaurant with my family and friends. I had passed it many times but had never had the chance to dine there. It had won a Best Restaurant award. When we entered—all eleven of us—we were impressed, but there was no one at the desk to greet us and we stood there waiting and waiting. When we were finally taken to our seats there was no explanation or apology for the delay.

That was only the beginning of one of the worst dining experiences you could imagine. We had one of the most stunning views in the world, in a well-appointed restaurant that had taken considerable thought and money to set up and had good food, but unbelievably poor customer service. We were ignored, we had to leave the table to find service, and the whole meal took over three hours—a long time with children. And nobody communicated with us or apologised for the delay.

We won't be patronising that restaurant again and we certainly won't recommend it to anyone. It will probably go broke or struggle financially, and the owners will blame the economy or something else—anything but the absence of a smile and a modicum of attention. As I say elsewhere— beware of the award winners!

You've got to have a ready smile, be genuinely friendly and want to go out of your way to please others. If this isn't you, don't waste your time in the personal service industry.

Sell unique and exclusive products

A very successful retail concept was launched a few years ago: business boomed as people flocked to the stores. If you needed to give someone a unique gift these stores were the place to go. They seemed to have items that weren't seen in other shops, and they always had an incredible array of new things that made shopping there a new experience every time. I was always curious to see what they would think of next. The staff would be enthusiastically demonstrating products as you entered the store and there was an air of fun and laughter. You could see on the customers' faces that they were having a good time spending their money—and that's the ultimate pointer to successful retailing.

Something began to change after one of the original owners died tragically quite young. Perhaps a lot of the creative product selection and development had been his genius, or maybe it was his leadership that they were never able to replace. Their catalogue got smaller and contained fewer new or exclusive products. The business was bought by a large public company that set about cutting costs. They began to close stores, and morale in the business dropped. Retailing is extremely competitive. Anyone can open a shop and put some products on a few walls. A key to successful retailing is to have products before anybody else, and to have a constant flow of them. In our businesses we developed exclusive products or negotiated exclusivity agreements with our suppliers. It gave us that profitable edge.

Chapter 8
On publicity

Over the many years Dick and I worked together, he demonstrated time and time again that the keys to getting publicity for your business are as follows.

Keep it simple and inexpensive.
Because we had no money for marketing we did simple things on the cheap. Nearly all the great publicity we got over the years cost us virtually nothing. Examples were the 'iceberg', the 'NO' sign, the Electronic Dick van and the Dickhead matches.

Create controversy
Almost every time we did something controversial it was successful at winning us media publicity, or the attention of our customers. The first example was our demonstration against Tandy. You can't be too conservative, for dull and boring news doesn't get attention.

Create genuine news
Dick created news by flying solo around the world by helicopter, and flying a balloon across Australia. These are things he liked to do, but adventures like that take a lot of time and money, and, by that measure, they aren't as effective as the unique, simple low-cost ideas.

Give them a benefit

We found that everybody likes a bargain, so if you can work benefits into your publicity, do it. For potential passengers on the flight to find Lasseter's gold reef we offered a share in the wealth. 'You Reap the Benefit!' was a slogan Dick used successfully in his electronics days.

The ultimate way to earn publicity

Dick would say that the ultimate, sure way of gaining media attention was to fail, or make a serious mistake. But neither of us would recommend it!

The pogo stick

The media are always looking for something entertaining or different, so if you have an idea you may be able to turn it into free publicity for your business. Dick first got on TV in 1974 with a petrol-powered pogo stick. He was sitting in his dentist's reception room one day and picked up a copy of the US magazine *Popular Mechanics*, in which there was an ad for the pogo stick. He sent away for one: it cost us US$120. When it arrived he called up newspaper journalist Peter Spooner and, tongue-in-cheek, told him he was going to bring in 10 000 of them to sell to housewives 'who could use them to shop at the supermarket'. He had no intention of doing any such thing, but he added, 'And imagine if you took one across the Harbour Bridge, what would the toll collector charge you?' Peter Spooner then came out to see us, and Dick took him and the pogo stick down to the local service station and yelled out to the attendant, 'Fill her up!' The bill came to two cents. In the

Dick on his petrol-powered pogo stick.

papers the story got bigger and bigger and in the end there were reports of Dick having bounced across the Harbour Bridge on the thing and having a confrontation with the toll collector about what he should pay. It was a myth: Dick never took it beyond the driveway, and the pogo stick was absolutely hopeless. You could do about two jumps on the thing before it backfired, nearly breaking your legs!

The pogo stick story attracted Chris Kirby, who had a TV show on late at night. Dick was at my girlfriend's place, where we were having a party, and he was plainly very nervous, as he had never been on TV before. On the way he cut out some 'Dickheads' from some matchboxes we gave away as promotional items and stuck them on the tiny petrol motor in case the camera zoomed in on it. The show was a success and later on he was invited on the *Mike Walsh Show*, and then he became a regular on the *Don Lane Show*. He got over his nervousness, was a bit of a larrikin and always had something unusual and different to show off, such as a heated toilet seat or a beer-powered radio, the alleged qualities of which he usually and cheerfully managed to enhance.

The NO sign

Dick was reading the Sydney *Bulletin* magazine and saw a cartoon of a burly businessman sitting at his desk with a timid little employee in front of him. Behind the businessman is a large NO sign surrounded by lights, and the big man says, 'Go ahead. Ask for something!' Dick loved it and had his own large sign set up in his office, with NO in black on a brilliant white background, and each letter out-lined with bright, incandescent light globes. Below this was a small sign, almost unnoticeable, that said YES, and below that was (MAYBE). He had a wonderful time with this sign, because he installed a plunger on his desk and when someone asked him for a decision and the answer was no, the NO sign would erupt with blinding lights and set off a very loud fire alarm bell, which could be heard all over the building. If the answer was yes, a small, almost inaudible beep would be heard and a tiny red globe would light up.

Everyone would smile when they heard the bell, and if the staff knew what their manager was asking, they would clap or boo, depending on which way they wanted the decision to go. It was a lot of fun and, of course, decisions were made quickly because Dick couldn't wait to push the switch. In the staff newsletter Dick reported: 'Rick Hallett has found that if he asks me a question in the negative, such as, "Well, Dick, is it okay with you if I don't take my holi-days next week?" I promptly push NO and he's off for a week. And Gary Johnston has threatened the next time I press the button he will throw a bucket of water over me ... I hope it's a hot day!'

Dick had someone ring the media to say that they had this terrible boss who had this NO sign and used it if you asked him for a pay rise or whatever. So the media phoned and asked him if it were true. Dick reluctantly said yes, 'but it wasn't one of those things he would want everybody to know about'. The media, of course, came out to his office anyway and did stories for the papers and TV about Dick and his mad NO sign. Great publicity.

'Go ahead. Ask me for something!'

Shortly afterwards Dick added a taxi meter to the arrangement. He was always anxious to maximise the number of things that he could fit into his day so time was of the essence, and he genuinely loathed time wasters. Outsiders who came to present a sales pitch were bemused or intimidated at first when confronted by Dick sitting in front of his NO sign, with a taxi meter on his desk pointing towards them. He would explain that they would have to pay the amount shown on the meter, 'as time was money', and the amount would be donated to charity. Dick would then swing the arm on the meter, it would start ticking and send the dollars turning. This was all done in fun, a big grin on Dick's face. It really did two things: it broke down the formality and communication was easier, and it got the message across 'let's not waste any time making this decision'.

When Dick Smith Electronics was sold to Woolworths I found it quite a contrast to pass through the large heavy doors into the formal, conservative and quiet sanctum of the managing director's office!

The Antarctic flights

The first 747 jumbo sightseeing trip to Antarctica of 13 February 1977 was an idea Dick had simply because he wanted to see Antarctica. He contacted Qantas and asked if they had ever thought of doing a flight. They laughed and said no one would ever want to go. Dick asked if they could charter him a 707 if he could get enough people to go. Qantas said they could, if he first put up $250 000, signed a contract and agreed to a non–cancellation clause. Dick knew he had to have a marketing angle to make it work and he came up with a pitch that said, 'Imagine one Monday morning when you get to the office and your friends ask you what you did on the weekend, and you say you flew to the South Pole!' Sunday's *Sun Herald* printed an article about Dick chartering the flight to the Pole and on Monday morning we came to work to find the switchboard, an earlier model that required the operator to plug in lines to extensions by hand, going absolutely berserk. All lines were jammed with incoming calls and our receptionist, Linda Turner, was going crazy trying to deal with them, but it was impossible. We hopped in and manned the phones, taking calls all around the office. Regular business became chaotic. People were bombarding our shops with calls when they couldn't get through to head office. It was hilarious.

"HOW LONG BEFORE YOU FIGURE OUT WHAT'S WRONG WITH THE COMPASS?"

How one newspaper cartoonist saw Dick's Antarctic flights ending.

Our logo on the T-shirts and commemorative medals. It helped keep Dick's name to the fore.

By 10 am the 707 was filled so Dick leapt on the phone and asked Qantas, 'Can we charter a 747 instead?' and they said yes, so we kept on taking bookings. In the end we filled two 747s.

We all flew down in just the Dick Smith Electronics South Pole Expedition T-shirts that we had had printed, and passengers got a quite large and heavy 'commemorative medal' around their necks. The medal read: 'Struck in commemoration of the Dick Smith Antarctic Expedition to the South Magnetic Pole and presented to a GALLANT COMPANION for outstanding comradeship on a long and eventful journey'. It was a laugh, although some of the recipients actually took the medal seriously. The 'long and eventful journey' took twelve hours.

Dick decided he would donate all the profit to charity and I think it was the beginning of his long-term commitment to raising money for charity. We ran nine Antarctic flights, raised a lot of money and got heaps and heaps of publicity for the business.

Lasseter's gold reef

After that, Dick got an idea to mount a 'search' for ill-fated explorer Lewis Harold Bell Lasseter's fabled, but claimed by some to be mythical, lost gold reef, reputedly near the West Australian/Northern Territory border. Dick advertised the search in the *Sydney Morning Herald*, with a typical Dick twist of imaginative marketing: you could go only if you signed a document that said you wouldn't blame Dick for all the problems you might experience, such as family break-ups and lifestyle changes, if you became immensely wealthy after the gold reef was found. He also declared that some people become corrupted as multimillionaires and if you thought there was a chance of that happening to you then you shouldn't come on the flight. One little old lady sent Dick $220, the fare for the flight, with a note saying she was too old to go but wanted a share of the wealth. (Dick sent the money back with a note saying to keep it, we would *give* her a share.) There was a Miner's Right certificate issued. We had Nose Peg, an Aboriginal tracker, sitting in the flight deck of the Qantas 747, and Dick organised media personalities to come along on the 6500 km, 10 hour flight. They arranged a competition as to who would find the gold reef first: Nose Peg the tracker; Lasseter's son Bob, who was on the flight; or the aircraft's inertial guidance system. Can you imagine a 747's inertial guidance system finding any sort of gold reef? It was all a fantastic lot of fun, the plane packed with 300 paying 'gold prospectors', their noses pressed to the cabin windows, allegedly searching for a lost gold reef. The drinkers at the Birdsville pub had assured us that they would stagger out and give us a wave if we circled the town at low altitude. During the flight the jumbo would fly close to the highly secret Pine Gap radio facility in central Australia, and when the media questioned Dick about that, he said that as the plane approached the area he would ask all prospectors to put away their binoculars and shut their eyes tight! The result of all this was another donation to charity and more publicity for the electronics business.

The iceberg

The 'iceberg' that was towed through the Heads into Sydney Harbour on April Fool's Day 1978 and made world headlines actually started out as a genuine idea. The newspapers had reported that an overseas company was seriously considering a feasibility study into towing an iceberg from Antarctica to Saudi Arabia to provide fresh water there. The proposal attracted much comment, and Gerry Nolan, who later became Mayor of North Sydney but was doing some work for us at the time, suggested to Dick that we tow a fake one into the harbour for April Fool's Day. The cost of towing in a barge covered with clear plastic filled with fire-fighting foam was $1200.

Iceberg off the Sydney Opera House!

The cartoonists played it cool.

Dick baited the press and had 2SM, then a leading morning station in Sydney, play along with the joke. There was even mention that the iceberg might be cut up and turned into 'Diksicles' or 'Dikblocks'. In the morning spectators lined the harbour foreshores to watch the 'iceberg' arrive. The joke went off with great good humour all round, receiving wide publicity. A few days later Dick flew to the United States to see if we could get the Midland CB radio agency. He was sitting in the office of the company president, John Lane, and there on his desk was the 'iceberg' story, with picture, on the front page of the *Chicago*

Tribune. Lane was impressed and said to Dick, 'You're obviously very dynamic!' He gave him the agency.

The Electronic Dick

That was the name painted, in huge letters, on the side of our delivery truck in 1978. It was also on the front, spelled backwards so it could be read in rear-vision mirrors, a new idea at that time. People said they saw our trucks with the cheeky signs 'running all around Sydney', but we had only that one truck! I can't remember getting one complaint about the wording, but when we opened our US branch in Redwood City, California, the Americans responded differently. The large banner on the side of our warehouse beside the freeway, reading 'The Electronic Dick is Coming!' wasn't up long before we got calls from the local city authority to say they were receiving complaints. But a lot of people did come into the shop to see us so it was good publicity too—and demonstrates how effective a simple gimmick can be in getting your company noticed.

The Missing Dick

At Australian Geographic we organised some coloured, life-sized, cardboard cut-outs of Dick holding an issue of the journal. We would stand them outside our shops. One day someone stole the cut-out outside our Hobart store, so the astute manager called the *Hobart Mercury,* which next day reported 'Dick Smith Goes Missing!' The story brought an amazing number of new customers into the store.

Dick became known as The Electronic Dick. Before Woolworth's bought the business we had our 'fleet' painted with this signage. Mike Middleton, our talented graphic designer, drew this cartoon for our in-house staff magazine.

The double-decker bus jump

The jump of a double-decker bus over seventeen motorcycles, aimed at topping famous stuntman Evel Knievel's record in jumping his motorcycle over seventeen double-decker buses, got world publicity too, and cost us only $2000 to do.

The day before the attempt, 29 August 1980, we were at a board meeting with Woolworths' managing director, Tony Harding, and other directors. Dick was signing contracts for the sale of Dick Smith Electronics. Towards the end of the meeting Tony asked Dick what he was up to and Dick said, 'Well, tomorrow I'm jumping over seventeen motorbikes in a double-decker bus.' Tony and the others looked stunned, as if they were wondering what they had done going into partnership with this fellow. I doubt they had

Up and over—Dick included!

ever run across someone like Dick. (After they knew us better I noticed that they really enjoyed our Dick Smith Electronics company culture and, I think, longed for some of our fun at Woolworths.) Anyway, adventurer Hans Tholstrup drove the bus and Dick was to play the uniformed conductor and to jump out before the bus took off over the ramp. The bus got going too quickly for Dick to jump; it cleared the bikes and landed with such an impact that Dick went flying, landing heavily in the aisle, badly bruised. Woolworths' brand-new partner hobbled from the bus, lucky to have escaped serious injury, but still grinning.

SkyLab is falling!

Nobody knew where pieces of SkyLab would crash to earth in 1979 but Dick decided to make it even more interesting by offering $5 million insurance cover for anyone hit by a piece of it while shopping in one of our stores. The cover generated a lot of entertainment for customers and staff and, of course, got the stores in the media right around the country.

The Smith Flight

The Smith Flight that Dick arranged with Qantas for 14 September 1980 was notable because to buy a seat on it your name had to be Smith. Enough Smiths to fill a 747 jumped at the chance. Qantas arranged that every crew member was a Smith, and there were even eight genuine Dick Smiths on board! The Reverend Len Smith came along to marry any Smiths who needed marrying and medallion maker Harry Smith struck a special medal to commemorate the trip.

Take-off was from Sydney's Kingsford Smith Airport and the first flyover was of Smith's Pinch, a sandhill in the Simpson Desert. We discovered that there were over 200 features bearing the name Smith in New South Wales alone, including twenty-two Smith Creeks. Dick told the story of how, as a small boy, his father told him that once everyone in the world had been called Smith, beginning with Adam and Eve Smith. It was only when they did something wrong that they had to change their name to something else. Dick said he was sure the story was true because he had spoken to lots of other Smiths in his time and they had all confirmed it. Again, all the money was given to charity, in this instance to The Smith Family, of course.

Bourke to Burketown Bash

Dick got the idea of the Bourke to Burketown Bash from a brochure about some fellows who had got some old cars together and driven them to Burketown, in Queensland's Gulf country. He thought it would be a great way of raising money for charity but added an idea of his own designed to attract Australian business people. He thought Australians part with their money for good causes as long as they're not looked upon as being 'do-gooders'.

Under Dick's rules, bribing and cheating your way to the finish line was permissible. Bribes had to be cheques made out to the Variety Club, but another competitor could outbid you with a bigger bribe. The biggest cheat was named the Ultimate Cheat and he received bonus points! Vehicles had to be at least twenty years old, and those with very low market value got bonus points. The rally started at the Sydney Opera House, with an 800 km run to Bourke, in outback New South Wales. The 'Bash' started when the vehicles left the bitumen and followed the Strzelecki Track to Innamincka and then through the horrific country of the Sturt Stony Desert. In that first bash in 1985, $240 000 was raised and Dick gave the concept to Variety for future events. A staggering $70 million has been raised in the seventeen years since. Variety has used versions of the idea worldwide.

The printed integrated circuit

Another April Fool's joke we did that gave everyone a lot of fun was a newspaper advertisement we took out launching the latest technology, the 'printed integrated circuit'. (We soon shortened this to 'printegrated circuit, or PRIC'.) We said all you had to do was sprinkle lemon juice on the drawing we printed, glue some wires to it and it became a radio. As part of the instructions we said that if you wanted to see the internal wiring you merely had to hold the ad up to the light. We bought some space on the reverse side of the page so that what you saw when you held it up was, 'April Fool!'. The response was really great. Although some people were upset that they couldn't get the 'radio' to work, most enjoyed the prank. One fellow wrote tongue-in-cheek to say he had even managed to get it to operate as a TV simply by hooking it up to a picture tube.

The bush office

On the four hectares of bushland in suburban Terrey Hills where he built the Australian Geographic Centre, Dick found a place for what he called his 'bush office'. It was nothing more than a few pieces of rough bush furniture standing uncovered in a small area of natural bush only 40 metres away from his real, well-equipped office with its two secretaries. He ran a cable out for computer, phone and intercom. The 'office' cost less than $1000. His first official visitor there was, by arrangement, Hazel Hawke, wife of the prime minister. When journalists sought an interview with him they would be led down the track to the bush office,

Hazel Hawke visits the 'bush office'.

to find Dick there amid the bird calls, a billy on the boil and, of course, they instantly had something to write about!

The Wilderness Couple

The *Alaskan Geographic* featured a story about a couple who went into northern Alaska to live on their own for a year. Dick, who had a childhood fascination for Robinson Crusoe, advertised for a couple willing to live alone in one of Australia's remote wildernesses, the north-west Kimberley coast of Western Australia. We offered to make their mortgage payments while they were away, but all the rest was up to them. Our search seemed to strike a chord of

Dick with the Wilderness Couple in the Kimberley.

escapism with the public, with more than 500 couples responding, including a number of doctors and lawyers yearning to escape. After many interviews we thought we had chosen a happily married couple, Michael and Susan Cusack, but after six months in the wilderness they told us they had, in fact, been living apart for several years and had applied in the hope that their year in the wild would result in their reconciliation. And so it did! The Cusacks were an outstanding couple, whose fascinating book on the adventure, *Our Year in the Wilderness* (1989), which we published, became a bestseller. All the publicity brought Australian Geographic a great deal of attention for very little.

Chapter 9

On managing people

Some are called to business, others are born to it

There are born business people just as there are gifted athletes, musicians and writers. I found you could try to teach the theory of leadership and business practice to some people but they would never catch on, while others had the instinct and capacity to lead or make a dollar.

Dick's mother once told me that the marketing skills that Dick later used so effectively were obvious at the age of seven. He bred more white mice than she wanted about the house, so Dick resolved the problem by putting up a notice at school: 'WHITE MICE FOR SALE, 10/6d at the Railway Pet Shop, 2 shillings from Dick Smith'. The mice were sold in a day. When later he was a student at the old North Sydney Technical High School he once took a rope to school, lowered it from a classroom window, and for a fee encouraged schoolmates to use it to escape Speech Day. *That* certainly sounds like Dick!

We were never able to make much of people who didn't have that natural talent for business. They ended up

costing us money and stress, and the experience wasn't fair to them either.

It's easier to hire than to fire

Think of the implications of a future downturn in business, for it's easier to put someone on the payroll than to remove them. We were very careful about putting on staff because we didn't want to have to sack anyone when business was tough, and we told people this. Because we ran lean, generally there was more work than everyone had time for, and we worked harder than the employees at most of our competitors.

How to stick your nose into other people's jobs

In many businesses, employees are encouraged to do only their own job and not get involved with or interfere in anyone else's. Thus they do not really know what's going on in the company beyond their own role. We wanted everyone to know what was going on, to know what everyone else was doing. We called this 'living the product'. Of course, the priority was for everyone to do their own work, and do it well, but if someone saw the likelihood of error developing somewhere or had a better idea of how something should be done, we encouraged them to express it. As a result, we had people who worked in the stores interested in errors that had happened in dispatch, or employees in the warehouse who would express concern if they learned a customer had not been looked after well in one of the shops. In an early issue of *Australian Geographic* some spelling errors had gone unnoticed despite proofreading, but they could have been picked up if others who had seen the proofs hadn't thought proofreading was not their responsibility. We encouraged people to take a wider view; in this instance the proofreader was asked to have as many people as possible look at the proofs. So, some of the staff not involved with editorial would take them home to read, and editorial encouraged this because it knew it would help them. *Australian Geographic*'s pages developed such a fine reputation for being error-free that some years later a reader wrote to say, tongue-in-cheek, he had finally found a spelling error, and that of course he knew we had inserted it deliberately to keep him on his toes!

It's a human thing to be protective of one's own work, so it took time and effort to make this change, but we did and it became part of the company culture. To do this you have to create an atmosphere that gives everyone confidence and a feeling of security in their job, so they are not defensive when others give advice or find errors. We praised people who embraced this mature approach. With this change we developed a unity that was good for business, for everyone felt involved in the management of the company.

A morale boost can boost productivity

One day Dick came bounding into my office at Dick Smith Electronics and said he would like to get a small sailing boat for the use of the staff. We talked about it and out of that arose an alternative plan to put in a swimming pool at our North Ryde distribution centre. The pool created a lot of fun. On hot summer days temperatures inside the warehouse would skyrocket, and many of the staff would cool down in the pool right alongside. They and their families also used it and the adjoining barbecue facilities at weekends. The pool wasn't that expensive to put in, but it increased productivity when we needed it most—at our peak Christmas period when temperatures were soaring. It proved that often simple things can build morale and make a big difference to a business.

Good people like high standards

We were very tough to work for and we told this to people up front before they decided to join us. Both Dick and I had very high standards and we had a very basic set of rules that everyone had to know about. They covered such things as honesty, theft, punctuality and procedures. I think discipline is necessary if a person is to continue to meet high standards day after day. We also found people responded better to the need to strive for high standards if they were given support and encouragement, and rewarded when work was well done.

Tolerate the employees who occasionally get emotional about the company's lack of performance or direction. They usually have a genuine interest in the business and want it to do well. They are often more useful than laid-back employees who accept lower standards. You need a few mavericks who tell you the truth about what's happening. From time to time they may be criticised by their colleagues as stirrers, but protect them to maintain a healthy company.

We had good supervision on all aspects of the business, so everyone knew we were interested in their work and in what they were achieving, and that provided motivation for them to continue. We had rigorous supervision of our shops and continual audits of the inventory. We sent out mystery shoppers to our stores to check how well the customers were being served. All facts in the *Australian Geographic* journal were checked by experts, sometimes to the frustration of our writers.

It took nearly a day for our supervisors to go through more than a hundred operation checks in our stores, and then each manager would be scored. What we noticed was that good people like aiming for high standards and good people like working for companies with high standards. The people who don't soon leave.

How do you find a new CEO? This ad shows how we did it.

There's nowhere for poor performers to hide in small companies although they can remain hidden for years in large organisations, and for a lifetime in large bureaucracies.

Keep the workforce on side

Although you must keep most of your workforce on side most of the time, you will never keep all of them on side all of the time. There are times when you will have to make unpopular decisions. I found that it was important to sell such decisions to the people who were most affected. If the decision was hard to sell to them, perhaps it wasn't so sensible after all.

Giving awards was another way of keeping the staff on side and morale high. At Dick Smith Electronics I used to carry a cheque book in my top pocket. The staff knew it as 'Ike's Magic Chequebook'. Whenever I saw something someone had done that I thought was special, I'd write out a cheque on the spot and hand it to them as a reward. It created some fun and showed we appreciated good work.

In the early days of Dick Smith Electronics we were having trouble getting our head office staff to get to work on time. As it was a retail company our shop staff had to get the shops open on time but they were then very frustrated if they called head office for help with a problem at, say, 9.10 am and the person they wanted hadn't arrived. We had a petrol bowser at work for the company delivery van. It was just outside the door where everyone bundied on in the morning. So I came up with a scheme that all names would go into a barrel and Dick would be asked to do a draw every week for a free tank of petrol for one person who had not been late all week. The drawing was done in front of everybody. I got the payroll officer to stand next to Dick with the time records showing who had been late.

Dick would dip his hand into the barrel and pull out names until he got someone who had been punctual. An advantage for the company was that the winner had to fill up his/her tank before 9.00 in the morning, so that those coming to work saw their colleague being rewarded.

Don't try to keep secrets, because you can't anyway

Dick and I never locked our offices or filing cabinets. Everyone knew our profits and expenses, how well or how badly we were doing. All our shop employees knew all our product cost prices. We found the more we told everyone the more committed and involved in the business they became. We encouraged them to ask questions. That way I believe there was less gossip, and fewer feelings of conspiracy or insecurity within the company.

Avoid management contracts

Some management contracts may work but I haven't seen many that did! If someone's not working out successfully, the company usually ends up making a huge payout to terminate their contract. In the cases that I have witnessed over the years, these termination payouts are very demoralising for the other staff. They send the wrong message: that failure is being rewarded. Contracts can create problems in other ways. If a person is not enjoying their work they are not going to perform well, so it's in the company's and their own interests to end it. You can't tie down a person's spirit in a contract.

Bonus schemes don't always work either

We tried a lot of bonus schemes for our people and most of them never worked! In fact, a lot of them were counter-productive. Don't think for a moment that people won't divulge their bonus to others, so assume there will be disclosures when allocating it. Some people will think they deserved more, or that others deserved less. There always seemed to be disputes, too, over the principles that decided the size of a bonus. We also found that many people who were very happy to get bonuses in the good times, lost motivation when bonuses were reduced in the tough times, so we lost staff just when we needed them most.

Promote staff and base salaries on merit

Sometimes we got it wrong but we tried to promote the best, and we paid the best performers well—and we let everyone in the company know that this was the way we did things. Our staff soon let us know when we had made a bad judgment, and this was good for the business too.

The best people we had came from within the company. They had usually started at the bottom and understood how the business worked. They also had a greater appreciation of their new position, because they had earned it. They were more loyal to the business and its culture and were less likely to change things that made the business work just for the sake of change. Because we knew each other well, we had fewer misunderstandings and we had lower staff turnover because others could see internal promotion was a fact.

If you need a good worker, ask a good worker

I found that the best employees in the company knew similar hardworking people of good character and could recruit them for me. In fact, I would offer them a reward to find a friend to fill a vacancy. If the new employee was still with us in twelve months I paid the 'recruiter' $300. The money was just a peripheral attraction: nobody wanted the embarrassment of recommending a dud so they got us the best people they knew, and we saved on our time and recruiting costs.

I learned there was another important advantage in getting our staff to recruit like-minded workers: such appointments helped preserve our company culture. It is quite surprising how one or two employees who disagree with your aims—at its simplest, with how you run the company—will create disaffection among other staff. This really can be serious if you employ managers inclined that way and they fill staff vacancies with people similarly carping or censorious. If the rot continues, your company culture will be destroyed.

Sack your staff after five years

Should you really sack your staff after five years? No, not really! But my experience is that many people give their best in their first five years of service, and it won't hurt for a boss to keep that in mind. Leave when you have given your best and let others leave too. You can also sometimes become less appreciative of colleagues, employees and suppliers over time. So, are you part of the problem? Ask yourself if familiarity has made you take others for granted. Stop and think occasionally about what your attitude was towards those employees, suppliers, customers and industry colleagues when you first met. Familiarity may have made you take them for granted. Rekindle your relationships. Really good people are hard to find. When someone was leaving our company I usually tried to see them. It was amazing what they would tell me about our business. They gave me an insight into what we could do to improve it, and sometimes I discovered we were losing someone we shouldn't and got them to reconsider.

Resolve internal rivalries

Infighting and internal rivalries waste time and money, and so you have to resolve them. At Dick Smith Electronics the retail division at times thought the wholesale division was taking its market share, and the wholesale division thought the mail-order division was taking theirs. At Australian Geographic the journal staff feared that retail was aiming to turn the journal into a vehicle for mass merchandising. I've seen companies set up internal profit centres with their own overhead structures and accountant, each centre manager competing with the other divisions for profit—and even for staff! Dick and I worked hard to reduce the politics in the companies by always trying to bring bickering back to 'What is the best thing here for the company overall?'

One of the products that did extremely well for Australian Geographic was the nine-volume *Australian*

Encyclopaedia. Dick came up with a plan that put an end to the retail/editorial rivalry. That year he announced a massive bonus, with everyone to share in it. When he handed out the cheques his message was that the bonus was only possible because the business had done extremely well—thanks to the sales of the encyclopaedia. There was a change of attitude by the journal's staff when they saw they were sharing in wealth generated by the company in all its sections. From then on there was a constant stream of editorial people to my office with new product ideas for the shops and the mail-order catalogue!

People *are* what they are

Never waste your time wishing that people could be different than they are. They seldom change in the way you want. When you put someone on, give them six months, and if they are not performing either accept them as they are or find somebody more acceptable. In our experience we might have to try two or three people in the more responsible roles before we got it right. Some managers found it hard to accept that their appointments weren't working out, and so kept the wrong person in the job. It cost the company far more to make the change down the track. Let your managers know this.

Whose idea is it anyway?

Dick had a knack of getting support for his ideas by occasionally having them credited to someone else. At a meeting he might discuss a problem and ask those present for advice, hoping someone in the group would come up with the solution he had already decided might work. When someone came up with it, Dick would leap up and yell something like 'Brilliant, what a fantastic idea, John!' and from that point it was John's idea, and it was always pushed as John's idea. Why would he do this? Because the boss can't always be satisfying his own ego. You're not going to get the same commitment from people if every time you get them together you merely announce your latest brilliant idea and instruct them to put it into action.

Chapter 10
On negotiating

Give little away

When negotiating give away as little of your position as possible. Any information you volunteer about your plans gives the other party an insight into your motivations and can be used against you. We were able to improve many deals because the other side kept talking, unnecessarily giving us knowledge that weakened their position and strengthened ours.

Think about long-term relationships

A business leader once told me to negotiate until 'you see the whites of their eyes' and never to appear anxious. He could have continued: 'but certainly never become arrogant or greedy—try to leave something for the other party'. Clinching a deal at a bargain-basement price may benefit you only for a short term. You don't want one of your major suppliers to cease supplying you or go broke because you screwed them on price. When I employed someone and got them to agree to a lower salary, it would often come unstuck down the track when the novelty of their new position wore off and they had to face the reality of paying their bills. There can be hidden resentment from people who feel you got the better of them, so look at the longer term in building relationships. It's surprising in business how often you have to negotiate with the same people but in new circumstances. Both parties will feel happier if they know there is some profit left in the deal for them. And after your negotiations are completed and the other party has agreed to your proposal, don't think about how much more you might have got: be satisfied.

Negotiating with your landlord

We purposely developed a reputation for being difficult to negotiate with, and when dealing with shopping centre landlords this was not merely effective, but necessary. When leases came up for rent review they knew we would be tough and that it would be tiring for them, as we would take up a lot of their time and effort.

We were forced into this by an unfair practice: as part of our lease agreements we had to disclose our sales figures every month to the shopping centre landlords. You couldn't rent space unless you agreed to this. The landlords said they needed the figures to determine how well their centre was going. Maybe they did, but they often used the sales results to pressure us for more rent. They would say we could afford to pay more because our rent-to-sales costs were too low compared with other retailers. Of course, we couldn't know if this were true without the figures, but it was true that if you did incredibly well your rent went up, and that if you did badly you could be ejected at the end of the lease.

I argued that the landlord should help us with the negotiations by disclosing how well they were doing with *their* income. They could start by providing us with the average rental income per square metre they were receiving, the number of vacancies in the centre, the number of retailers not paying rent and how much the smaller specialty shops were subsidising the major anchor tenants. I would point out that disclosing their rent figures would help us retailers decide whether we were getting value for our rent money.

Not surprisingly, I never got answers but we found they usually came in with fair offers, or avoided dealing with us altogether. I did feel, though, for the small family businesses whose owners had invested their life savings in their shops and had to battle these shrewd, tough property owners.

Doing business with Kerry Packer

I had a memorable encounter with Kerry Packer, Australia's richest man, when Dick and I went to see him about the possible sale of Australian Geographic. Of all the people I have met in business, I found him to be the most impressive, sharpest and shrewdest. I also found the fellow incredibly likeable, witty and dynamic.

Kerry had telephoned Dick out of the blue and asked if he was interested in selling his business. Dick had recently expressed a thought, privately and certainly not to Kerry, that he was ready to try something new. Dick wasn't that keen to talk to Kerry, as he had once approached him for advice on film making and their meeting hadn't gone that well. Anyway, Dick thought *Australian Geographic* readers would be upset if the proudly independent journal were to be sold to the powerful Packer media group. However, I was excited at the chance to see Kerry Packer at what he does best—wheeling and dealing—and encouraged Dick to at least hear what he had to say. We also recognised that it might be to our advantage if we were negotiating with other potential buyers and were able to say we had been having talks with Kerry Packer.

At the Australian Consolidated Press headquarters in Park Street, Sydney, we were met in the foyer by James Packer, who took us up to his father's office. Kerry greeted us and introduced us to Brian Powers, who sat down quietly in the corner and took notes during our whole discussion.

It was clear from the beginning that Kerry thought Dick wanted to quit the business and would part with it for a bargain. Dick explained that the business was making a fortune, which it was, and if he sold it he would have to find alternative investments to give him the return that he was getting. He mentioned that he would need to acquire at least a $60 million commercial building to give him a clear 10 per cent net return.

Kerry snapped, 'What do you want f----ing property for?' Quickly turning to Brian Powers, he asked, 'Do we own any f----ing property?'

Brian replied no, and Kerry leaped to his feet and yelled, 'F---! We own *this f----ing property*, Brian! How much is this f----ing building worth?'

Brian didn't know, so Kerry told James to go and find out how much 'this f----ing building' was worth, upon which James hurriedly left the office.

I sensed that Kerry was ready to do a deal with Dick then and there, and that James would return with a figure of $70 million, Kerry would offer the building to Dick at a valuation of $60 million, a handshake would follow and the deal would be done.

To my surprise James quietly returned to the office to say everybody was at lunch and no one could be found to give him the valuation. So Kerry suggested he give Dick shares in return for Australian Geographic. Dick had always avoided owning shares, preferring property, and wasn't enthused at all by that idea.

I began explaining the retail and publishing parts of our company to Kerry, how the synergy between the two worked and the potential there was to expand the business. I told him that the average sales in one of our shops was around $10 000 a square metre per annum, when he turned to me and said, 'I don't know anything about f----ing retail, but that must be f----ing good, because if it wasn't you wouldn't be f----ing telling me, would you?' He was right, of course.

I left the building knowing that nothing would come of the meeting, as Kerry was too shrewd to pay what the company was worth. I suspected that he only bought when he got a bargain and sold when he got top dollar. Yet I was surprised, too, when I left thinking I could work for Kerry. I liked his direct, speedy, no-nonsense approach to doing business. And later on I had a couple of meetings with James and decided they were two very impressive business-men.

Negotiating and winning

You are in the best bargaining position when you don't want what you are bargaining for. This seemed to happen to us when we lost interest in what we were pursuing—a shop site, a product, an agency, real estate. I found that when our interest waned the offer usually got better, and the more cooperative the seller became.

You can usually feel when you are winning. There is increased awareness, an intuitive sense—possibly developed through experience—that helps you judge whether the situation has winning possibilities. When that happens, everything comes together perfectly.

Chapter 11
On honesty

Truth in business

There's not a lot of truth in the business world, and the sooner you discover this, the better a businessperson you will be. Behind just about every deal there is a fake facade. Just about every business presentation—whether by employees or employers, and whether addressed to a department, the board or the shareholders' annual general meeting—has a gloss to make things look better or worse, depending what benefits the presenter most. We learned that nothing is ever as bad as it first appears—or as good!

Whom can you trust?

Whom should you trust in business? Nobody. Early in my career I was conned by someone I employed to drive the company's delivery van. He was one of my best workers and he had a terrific attitude towards the business. One day I had a call from the real estate agent who managed the apartment our employee occupied, to tell me he had gone over to collect the man's back rent, found the door unlocked, and would I come and meet him there? The apartment was stashed with thousands of dollars' worth of goods that should have been delivered to our shops and still unopened mail-orders that should have gone to the post office. I was young, it was the first time my trust had been betrayed and I was *devastated*. But it was certainly not the last time I was taken in, and I came to learn that usually the persons stealing from our business were those least likely to be suspect. Quite often they were the brightest, hardest working employees, including managers, and generally it was not financial pressure that made them steal, it was greed. Checks and balances in your business should go right to the top. Our company auditor checked up on the things that I did, and I was happy for Dick to see that I, too, was accountable.

Past performance can be a clue to the future

People seem rarely to change their habits, whether good or bad. We had a company rule that all previous employers were to be contacted for references and all dates of employment checked, but we failed badly once when we were in the middle of the CB radio boom and could hardly keep up with mail-orders.

I had a call from a customer complaining he had not received his radio, so I went down to the mail-order department to check with the manager. There was no trace of the order, despite our strict cross-referencing system. The customer then told me he had given the order to the same manager at a CB radio club meeting, and he had a receipt on a Dick Smith letterhead.

I confronted the manager. Yes, he had taken the order, but kept the money and 'hadn't got round' to dispatching the goods. Investigation revealed that he had done this on a number of occasions, personally packing the goods himself but keeping the money. What's more, he was known to the police. We looked back at our records to find out why we hadn't picked this fact up. We had checked all references but one. He had said on his employment application that he had worked on his father's country property for a number of years, and we had not verified it. He had, in fact, been in gaol.

The surprising thing was that he later got a job as sales manager of a company that distributed goods to us, among others. Nobody from that company had called us for a reference.

Take your garbage to the cleaners

At the end of the week at Dick Smith Electronics many of us would go to the local for a drink. One evening Dick joined us, and he and I listened approvingly as one of our enthusiastic young employees told us about which electronics kits he found were selling well, which kits had potential to sell better, and which lines he thought should be discontinued. He later excused himself and left, remarking cheerfully that it had been a long and busy week.

Dick left not long afterwards, his route home taking him past our store. As he drove by he was surprised to see the same enthusiastic young fellow standing next to the big steel garbage bin outside the shop with a heavy box, and he watched as the young fellow carried the box to his car and put it in the boot. Dick hurried over and demanded to see what was in it. The box was filled with electronic goodies the fellow had tossed into the bin during the day!

We then put in place a procedure to check garbage bins regularly and, of course, we let everybody know we did. When I opened Dick Smith Electronics in California years later I adopted the same procedure, and let everybody know about it. One day after closing, the warehouse supervisor came to tell me he had found a carton of radios in the garbage bin. I called the police, who very professionally decided to set up a van equipped with surveillance video in the car park that night. Around midnight the hidden camera recorded the arrival of a vehicle, one of our employees alighted and removed the carton from the bin. His arrest devastated the staff, as he was well liked and they felt their trust had been betrayed. Again, it shows you just cannot predict who will defraud you or when.

But this is not something you need dwell on, other than by seeing to it that tight anti-theft measures are in place and by talking to your people about temptations. Thousands of fine, honest people worked with us over the years. Only a handful of people were not honest.

Short-term gains bring some people unstuck

Opportunities to be less than honest in your dealings with people occur daily because of the pressures on you to make things look good to immediate advantage. In the long term this brings many people unstuck. The best policy is always to be straightforward, and not to waver from it. Others' trust in you is something of incredible value in your career, and it is built up steadily.

I have observed an incredible inclination by lazy and/or dishonest executives to rort their company through long lunches, padded business expenses and other such abuses. The pity is that if they focused their energies on getting a better return for the shareholders they would themselves be better rewarded in material terms—and become more highly regarded.

Are the directors looking after you?

If you're a shareholder in a public company, don't think the directors and senior management are looking after your interests: more likely they are looking after theirs. How many AGMs are taken up with approvals for new share options and bigger remuneration packages for directors and executives? Because public companies are under a lot of pressure to look good to their shareholders, some executives plan only for the short term to get the profits and share price up, quite often only long enough to get their bonus. For us, as a private company, it was much easier to do what we wanted to do, and that was also best for the company in the long term.

Chapter 12
On making and saving money

Nothing booms forever

There will always be competition. Just when you think you are winning, someone will crop up and try to take your market share. Get used to it: that's the free enterprise system. Your market is constantly changing; your share increasing or decreasing. So, while business is booming, prepare for the downturn. At both Dick Smith Electronics and Australian Geographic we had amazing cycles as we rode boom products. Plan for the inevitable downturns in business by building a buffer for sales to drop, and watch your fixed costs too.

Paying your bills promptly can be good for business

If we had a supplier with a top-selling product and there was a shortage caused by brisk demand, they'd supply what stock they had to our company first, rather than to a company that made them wait for payment. If small companies provided unique products we even had a cheque waiting for them on delivery. This helped their cash flow and

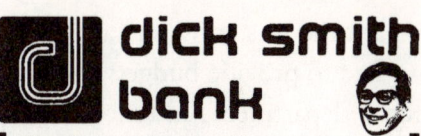
Our ad for Australia's lowest priced bank appeared in the *Sydney Morning Herald*. It failed to inspire the banks but we did get a lot of publicity.

encouraged them to supply any new products to us before our competitors.

You're rarely on a winner with annual budgets

If you come in over budget you're criticised for aiming too low, and if you set your targets high and fail to reach them, you're damned as a loser. You can't win. Annual budgets also cost the company money. In one of the public companies we worked with, there would be a mad panic just before the end of the financial year for managers to spend their expenses budget for fear it might be cut the following year. That money could have gone back into reserves and been better used, or added to the shareholders' dividend.

I found budgeting a great time waster. When, as part of a large public company, we had to provide budgets, we collected all the guesses from our departments and shops. Then senior management guessed what guesses were good and what guesses were bad, and together we guessed what the final guesses would be. The guesses then went to the company budget meetings, from where they were sent to the board and from there, I guess, the guesses went to the shareholders.

Employ the meanest, most miserly accountants you can find

Tell everyone the accountants' only thrill in life is to save a dollar, and make them the reason why you can't spend the money everyone wants you to. (Good luck in your search for these paragons.) Dick and I both grew up without a lot of money so we were incredibly conservative about spending, and we hated waste. Dick's attitude was that if we made lots, we could give some to charity.

Avoid borrowing money if you can

Dick's father had always warned him about the dangers of borrowing money, but Dick's companies never had any borrowings because at the beginning of the business nobody would lend him any. No bank would even talk to him because he lived at home with his parents and his car-radio business was in the basement of the Big Bear supermarket in Sydney's Neutral Bay, where just about everyone had gone broke. This turned out to be a great discipline for

Staff organised this cartoon to illustrate what they thought of cost controls at Australian Geographic

the business after it started to grow, because we had to be cautious and creative with the funds available. Over all the years I worked with Dick I never went to a bank to negotiate a business loan. All our growth was funded by internal cash flow. If we didn't have the cash for it, we didn't buy it.

Sign all your company's cheques

I found this an incredibly effective way to get a grasp on what the company was spending. Countless times I was able to put a stop to waste before it went any further, and my signing all the cheques acted as a deterrent to excessive spending because everyone knew that I would see what they had spent. It also encouraged people to save money, and I complimented those who negotiated a good deal. One day I congratulated our buyer on his frugal expenses during an overseas buying trip. He had spent only $22 on food in four days. He accepted the compliment, but as he turned to leave the office I caught a smile. He then confessed he had picked up a gastric bug there and hadn't been able to eat a thing for a week!

Have a tough purchasing policy

All the products we wanted to buy had to give us a targeted gross profit margin, or we wouldn't buy them. It was surprising how many suppliers lowered their selling prices to make our threshold.

Your staff won't watch costs if you don't

We attended many international trade fairs and always flew economy class. And we made sure all our people knew it.

Don't try to stock everything

We didn't stock every item possible, not even if a customer asked us for it. We limited the number of different products to a specific maximum and everyone on staff knew what that was. If company buyers wanted to add a new product to the range, they had to discontinue a slow seller. In this way we kept less capital tied up in inventory and our buyers didn't get oversold by overenthusiastic suppliers.

Think profit, not sales

It always surprised me how many business people judged how well their business was going by looking only at the sales turnover. It's easy to get sales: it's the cost of getting them that's important. Many times we were making a lot more profit than large retailers doing hundreds of millions of dollars' more business. When I was approached by people with great products or venture ideas they said would 'add lots of sales to the business', the first thing I did was start from the bottom profit line and work up the profit and loss statement. We wanted to know how much profit the product would add to the business—the sales were secondary. When you start focusing on profit, your people will too.

I think the fundamental fact that a business has to make a profit was lost on many people involved with the dotcom explosion and subsequent bust. I was invited to join a board planning to float an Internet retailing company. I went to a meeting where the business plan was aired and I listened attentively before asking first, what the current monthly overheads were, then what the expected sales for the first week were and, finally, when they thought they would make a profit. By that time, Dick and I had had long experience of mail-order, and I believe there is very little difference between producing a catalogue and displaying your goods on the Internet. You still have to have great products to get someone to buy, you still have to have the products in stock, and you still have to turn the orders around efficiently and quickly. All this is costly, requiring extremely good systems and very good people to run them.

I was stunned to be told that before they opened the doors for business this company's overheads were already $400 000 a month. They expected to do $70 000 business in the first week, and they seemed vague about when they would make a profit. I told them they would be lucky to do $7000 business in their first week, that I didn't think they would ever make a profit and that as soon as their capital injections stopped they would fold. One of the partners said, 'Ike, things have changed. In this new era you may never have to make a profit. It's how much potential you have to make a profit some time in the future that's important.' The business never listed.

'Bye, big spender

I found there were always many more people coming into my office with ideas on how to spend money than people with ideas on how to make money or save it. When they wanted approval to spend, their biggest problem was to convince us. After a while the message got through. Also, everything costs more to complete, and longer to complete, than people anticipate, so you needn't be fooled by all those who will insist otherwise.

The cost of disillusionment

Customer or employee disillusionment with a company isn't generally felt immediately. It develops over a period of time, increasing its pace until it overwhelms the business. Sales drop, overheads rise and the business goes broke.

When it happens it is amazing how those in charge blame everything for it but their own mismanagement.

Chaos and the making of money

It seemed that whenever we were in the most chaos we were making the most money. Whenever we couldn't get enough product to sell, enough employees to ship the product and the entire company was stretched beyond capacity, profits were higher than ever before. It seemed that whenever we were well organised, had time to ponder as the business coasted, we were making the least money.

Chapter 13
On communicating successfully

Who reads your office memos and emails?

At one time I used to send regular memos to all our staff. After a while I suspected that no one was reading them, so one day I dropped into the middle of my memo a line in parenthesis reading, 'Phone me if you are reading this and I'll give you $20'. Nobody phoned.

Keep your door open

Dick and I always maintained an 'open door' policy: anyone could walk into our offices at any time. In neither company did we ever have a stop-work meeting. We listened to, had time for and mixed with all levels of employees. Everyone knew they had access to management. We worked with our office doors open and closed them only on rare occasions. Employees didn't need an appointment to see us and there were constant interruptions from people wanting advice or decisions, but we knew this small frustration was outweighed by the importance of good, quick communication to the business. We had people of all ages, from all levels of the business, popping in and out when they got a good idea or when they were unhappy about something and wanted to criticise the way we were running the company. If we listened to employees, they didn't need a union delegate to listen to their complaints. We also learned that if we listened to customers' suggestions and ideas we made more money, and if we listened to their complaints they didn't have to seek out the Department of Fair Trading.

Assume everyone's an idiot unless proved otherwise

A few months after I joined Dick he told me to assume everyone's an idiot unless proved otherwise. He was only half-joking. His comment helped me communicate better and not assume that somehow everyone would, at all times, have a clear picture of what I expected them to do. A lot of the worst errors we made over the years were caused by an *assumption* that someone was going to take responsibility for something, but nobody had told them. (Warning: Despite Dick's early advice, I confirmed this truism through hard personal experience.)

Talk to your people

Some of our best ideas came from our employees. I'm amazed how often senior management stay stuck in head office, insulated from reality and rarely visiting or mixing with their employees. Recently I visited a store that was part of a once very successful chain and I spoke to the store manager about why he thought the group was falling behind. He knew, and summed it up succinctly. He spoke about the lack of marketing, shortage of unique and exclusive products, the loss of good people because of low morale, and a growing feeling of hopelessness. He said standards were dropping throughout the group because of a decline in discipline and attention to detail, and poor service to customers. I asked this manager if he had spoken to senior management on these critical issues. Yes, he had spoken to his immediate supervisor, who told him to stop whingeing. Had anyone called him or visited him from head office? No. I knew exactly what needed to be done for that company. There had to be a clean-out of senior management, middle management needed to be read the Riot Act and strong leadership had to be introduced at CEO level. There would be some useless directors on the board too. Here was a man who had clear views about the company, but nobody was paying attention. I could just hear top management analysing the company's problems during tedious and lengthy meetings, probably with the help of expensive outside consultants, and finally blaming the economy, the changing marketplace, the GST—anything but the real problem, which they could identify by listening to their own people.

Dick's candid video show

Dick Smith Electronics was booming and it was becoming impossible for us to visit our growing number of shops as often as we should. Video was just becoming available at a sensible cost, so I got the idea of having Dick record a weekly video show for the shop staff. We would display new products we were planning to stock and indicate a proposed retail price for them. Copies of the video would go off to the shops with a printed sheet of all the products shown, and staff members were asked to vote on whether we should stock them. The results were presented on the next video. We told the buying department they could purchase only what the shops had voted for. We used the same system with the Australian Geographic shops. We didn't buy a thing without our employees' approval and they loved telling us what we could and couldn't do. They also became very committed to selling the products they had selected.

It wasn't long before use of the video was widened. Staff would send memos to us with ideas, complaints or queries, and Dick and I addressed these matters on the small screen, explaining what was being done. The sender of the message was always identified. If someone did something great we would reward them, over the video. I took the camera with me all over the country and interviewed our top salespeople, or recorded something I had seen that I thought would work in another shop. We would sometimes take the camera into our warehouse to show the packing procedures and the top packers, or interview outside business leaders for useful comments or inspiration. We got free promotional plugs on the *60 Minutes* television show and on the front page of the *Australian Financial Review*. These resulted in calls from a number of big companies that wanted to come and have a talk about how the idea worked. I don't know if any of them put it into practice.

Their eyes appeared to glaze over when I explained that it was really great having the staff making the decisions.

Our 100th video show was quite memorable. Unbeknown to Dick or me, somebody organised a girl from Boobs and Bubbly to come and present Dick with a bottle of celebratory champagne while he was sitting at his desk. She was topless as she entered the video room. Dick looked round in the middle of his spiel to see what all the commotion was about and found the lady leaning over him. He managed to regain his composure and mutter something like, 'We're fully abreast of the times!'

Tell it like it is

There are times when you need to be *very* direct with somebody on the staff. Your politically correct determination to be a diplomat can sometimes confuse the message, so the person targeted is left mystified or convinced there is no real problem. Instead of filling out long appraisal forms and scoring a person's performance, I'd sometimes simply call the person in and say, 'Sorry, but you're not working out here, and I'm going to tell you exactly why.' In a few sentences I would spell it out. Then I would tell him or her to go away and try out what we'd talked about,

The ads for Dick Smith Electronics knew just how to communicate with our customers.

and that we would review the situation the next week. A lot of the management books say you shouldn't be as direct as this, but it certainly worked for me. I found that people accepted being told just where they stood. Nor is it just the 'problem people' who can benefit from the direct approach. When I noticed someone doing something really well, I'd phone or drop into the shop or their office and say, 'I'm calling to tell you that I liked the way you did this or that.' I never had any complaints about that, either.

Chapter 14

On successful business practices

Send management to the barricades

At Dick Smith Electronics we rostered head office management to visit the shops. They hated leaving the comfortable confines of their offices, so we made a point of sending the roster to each shop manager and I soon heard if there was a 'no show'. The shop staff were especially delighted if they had someone from head office in their shop when there was a customer complaint, and they'd drag the embarrassed worthy over to deal with it. The roster took the management out of their comfort zones to face reality, but it also resulted in them developing an admiration for the sales people, it greatly improved communication, it fostered teamwork and it reduced the number of mistakes.

Red-Letter Days boost morale

One afternoon Dick announced there would be no work at Australian Geographic next day, but everyone was to turn up at 8.30 for 'a mystery tour'. A waiting coach took us to the airport, where we boarded an old wartime Dakota aircraft that was painted bright red. It flew us to the Hunter

Valley vineyards, where a red double-decker bus was waiting to take us to a marvellous lunch and wine-tastings. It was a Red-Letter Day, talked about for months.

Avoid litigation if you can

Litigation is costly and it will take your attention off your business. If you run your business ethically and do the right thing by people, it's unlikely you will end up a defendant, but if you are considering becoming the plaintiff, think about how valuable your time is and whether the exercise is worth it. We were able to settle a lot of things before they got serious by just sitting down with the other party and being sensible and reasonable about the issues.

On one occasion Apple Computers wrote to us to say legal action would be taken against us because the software for the disk controller in the Apple-compatible computer we were selling was a copy of theirs. I didn't call our solicitor but sought out Apple's managing director and said that Dick Smith Electronics was an ethical company, and if we found any evidence that the software had been copied we would immediately withdraw it. We both seemed to be of the opinion that we could arrive at a reasonable outcome.

I contacted the manufacturer in Hong Kong. Had they copied the software? They emphatically denied they had and were offended that they were being questioned. I said I wanted them to come to Sydney so we could print out the software line-for-line and compare it with Apple's, with Apple engineers present. No problem, they said.

So, one Sunday all of us sat down with the engineers. Almost immediately it became clear that our software was a copy. We said we would instantly withdraw it. We had been misled, but we were dealing with Apple's David Strong, a fair and reasonable executive, and thus avoided an expensive legal case that no doubt we would have lost. We also decided it would be too time-consuming to take action against our supplier.

There are times when you have no alternative but to protect your interests, and you must, but don't let yourself be urged on by ambitious lawyers who say you can't lose. How often do they say you can't win?

Learn from others

When Dick thought about starting *Australian Geographic* he studied similar journals worldwide—*Canadian Geographic, National Geographic,* Italy's *Airone,* Germany's *Geo,* and *GEO* and *Walkabout* in Australia. After much discussion with publishers, editors and printers, he took good ideas from each magazine. You can see some of them—such as the story themes we selected, the extended picture captions, the large page size and high printing quality—in the early issues of *Australian Geographic.* When we later started the Australian Geographic stores I was inspired by the American stores The Nature Company, Natural Wonders and Smith & Hawkins. I visited wildlife, environmental and outdoors shops around the world and also got inspiration from their catalogues. From these beginnings we were able to develop our own creative input—because, of course, to be unique and competitive you have to have your own ideas too.

Surf the waves

If you can seek out a good product or a new trend before everyone else, you'll ride the profit margins at the top of the wave. (But get off the wave before it dumps you!) In 1975 Dick Smith surfed colour TV, in 1976 FM radio, in 1977 CB radio, in 1979 TV games and in the 1980s the personal computer. In the late 1980s and 1990s the wave was the growing interest in our Australian environment, and thus *Australian Geographic*.

Don't make promises

We learned through tough experience that promises made to customers or employees sometimes couldn't be fulfilled, despite our best intentions. You just cannot predict what future events will impact on your promise. A supplier would promise delivery of a product in huge demand on a certain date. We would tell our customers in good faith, only to be let down. An employee eager to please would promise a product could perform in a certain way, and it wouldn't, or would promise to return telephone calls and not do so—not because he didn't intend to but because he got caught up with other customers. There was the promise that 'I'll dispatch your mail-order by this afternoon' that didn't happen because of some glitch in the packing room; or the promise that 'I'll call you as soon as that new product comes in' that wasn't followed through. A manager with good intentions would promise a promotion or pay rise to an employee under certain conditions, but circumstances would change and he couldn't deliver. No matter how much justification there was for the change, the employee felt let down.

After experiencing the negative fallout from too many failed promises, we decided to train our staff not to promise anything to anyone. It had really great results. We had happier customers and employees when we explained why we couldn't make a promise. And their expectations were lowered, so when something better than expected happened, they were especially pleased.

Make your business more cost effective

We made our Australian Geographic business more cost effective by combining the publishing, mail-order, wholesale and retail divisions to maximise sales and profits.

The company began as a magazine publisher, producing the one journal, *Australian Geographic*, and building a subscriber base of more than 200 000. We used the material that was being created for the journal, such as maps and photographs, in a growing range of other products. A photograph or piece of artwork might also be reproduced on a greeting card, stationery, gift paper, an address book, a diary or a wall poster, or in the pages of the *Australian Encyclopaedia* or one of our growing range of popular books and annuals. This not only gave us exclusive high-profit products but reduced the cost of artwork, photography and editorial input for the journal itself. These Australian

Geographic products were then sold through the Australian Geographic shops, which publicly fostered the philosophy of the journal and the Australian Geographic Society.

We were then able to sell subscriptions for the journal to customers in the shops, which were located in high-profile shopping centres, and further build our public image. Our subscribers were able to meet the people behind the journal and were given benefits in the shop that were exclusive to subscribers. We produced a mail-order catalogue full of these products and many others aimed at our subscribers' interests, such as birdwatching, astronomy, travelling and camping. This catalogue accompanied the journal when it was posted to subscribers, so it 'free rode' the post, and we had to pay only for the printing. Our subscribers became our loyal shoppers, and when they received their latest catalogue they ordered products by mail or came to shop in person.

The synergy of the business was further improved when Fairfax bought the company and we were able to get in-house rates for advertising, and so advertised more often and less expensively. Marketing inserts in Fairfax publications for the journal, calendars, books and other products all built further public awareness, and our profits.

Pay your customers to help you run your business

We used to offer a reward to any customer who spotted an instance of thieving in our shops and told us about it. We offered a $50 reward for our catalogue readers who sent us product suggestions that we later took up—we had people sending us things from all over the country. They loved participating in the business. In the shops we provided a barrel and distributed a circular inviting customers to 'Tell us what you think!' There was space on the circular for them to give us their opinions, ideas, criticisms, whatever, and they did. When we made the $50 reward offer for new products for the first time in a small announcement in the Australian Geographic catalogue, we included the name of our buyer, Richard Wood. His mail had to be wheeled in on a trolley the following week! Probably the most unusual item suggested was a kangaroo scrotum, which a manufacturer had turned into a bag for loose coins.

Think before employing friends or relatives

As a manager, you are in a difficult position if you have friends or relatives in the business. There can be jealousy, politics and general gossip if other staff perceive the boss's friends or relatives are being promoted or rewarded. I made it quite clear to people that, like everybody else, I had good friends among my colleagues, but that as manager I had two personalities—one social, the other work—and at work my friends would be treated the same as everyone else.

Well, so much for the theory! No matter how impartial I thought I was, there were times when some people wanted to see it differently. Most times when we hired friends, or commissioned them to do work for us, it ended in disaster, or at least damaged relationships. A friend of mine who owned a very successful retail business for many years recently told me that he had pinpointed the start of its decline to the date when he involved his children in it. It can be difficult, but if you want to keep friendships and strong family relationships I think it's best not to involve them in your business.

And here's another point on friends. A number of years ago I was on a plane in America and the in-flight magazine had a story on a magazine editor. The editor was commenting about the huge number of story submissions she received for publication and how she had to reject so many of them. One of the things rejected authors most commonly said to her was 'But all my friends have read the story and they think it's great', to which she would reply, 'And that's why they're your friends!' I thought that was brilliant and it has stuck with me ever since. When you seek advice or an opinion from friends and family keep that thought in the back of your mind.

Post your company goals

Post your company goals around your business so everyone knows what the business is aiming to do. Make them achievable, measurable and shared. This helped to make our organisation focused and gave us all a purpose.

Do it now—do it in parallel!

One of Dick's favourite sayings was 'Do it in parallel'. It makes sense to do it now because I found you never seem to have more time than you do right now. Something else will take the place of what you want to do now, and getting back to the previous task is much harder as the motivation diminishes.

OUR COMPANY GOALS

1 To manage and operate an electronic retail company with higher professional standards than any other company in the world.

2 To have 25 stores by June 30th, 1983, with a turnover of $25,000,000.

3 To expand to North America and have our first outlet by 1985.

At Dick Smith Electronics we posted the goals prominently in the workplace.

'Why don't you do it in parallel?' was one of the things I picked up from Dick as a 20-year-old when I grumbled that I didn't have enough time to do something. Dick was very skilled at this. He would always have an amazing array of things happening in his life at the one time, and what he couldn't do he would quickly delegate to others.

Don't waste time on corporate plans

I found it hard to write corporate plans. We could never predict what was going to happen from month to month, let alone from year to year. When Woolworths bought out Dick Smith Electronics, one of the first things they asked for was a corporate five-year plan. I explained we were a small, innovative company selling technology products and that we changed our plans almost weekly because these sorts of products changed so quickly. They said our division had to have this document, just like all their other divisions, so I spent a week writing fiction instead of making money for Woolworths' shareholders.

Limit reports

One day at Dick Smith Electronics the IT manager came to me asking for a bigger computer and more staff because of the growing number of weekly reports that needed printing and distribution. I asked for a list of reports and where they were going. There were thirty-five. I took my pen and crossed out half of them, and said, 'Let's see how long it takes for someone to scream.' We ended up with the existing computer, fewer staff and just twelve reports.

Keep rules to a minimum

Remember every rule and procedure you put into your business will have to be supervised, and this costs money and takes management's attention. Just because you wrote something in a manual doesn't mean it will be followed, so if you are not prepared to spend time defending or enforcing the rules, they will be broken. The rules also have to make sense to get staff support. We had company procedures that had to be strictly followed but we kept them to the bare minimum and made sure there were good reasons for having them. And as soon as someone provided a good reason for changing a rule, we'd change it.

Keep things simple

Often I would be sitting in a meeting with Dick while he heard somebody's proposal when he would suddenly ask a single, very pertinent question, and that would be the end of the meeting: there was nothing left to discuss. I've observed this trait in other top business leaders. They quickly grasp a complex issue, reduce it to the most basic terms and waste no more time on it.

One such mind belonged to Paul Simons, the former Woolworths chairman who was instrumental in turning that company around from its perilous situation in the 1980s. I once tried hard to encourage him to write a book about it, and even lined up a publisher, but Paul said, 'What I did was so simple it could be written on a single sheet of paper!'

Dick and I would often laugh together when someone from outside the company would ask Dick why he sold Dick Smith Electronics, and Dick would say it was because he couldn't fit all the shops with their weekly sales on an open spread of the school exercise book he used. He would claim that he couldn't read a balance sheet, and I don't think he could, but that's not to say he couldn't learn if he wanted to—he was just never interested in knowing how. He would say to me, 'Ike, isn't it quite simple? If you buy something for $1 and you sell it for $2 and you keep your costs low you must make a profit.'

I was at a meeting with our firm of auditors, discussing the company's performance, when Dick concluded the meeting by saying, 'But we must be making money if we've paid cash for everything, paid our taxes and we've got all this money in the bank we didn't have before.' It was difficult to argue with that logic.

Dick got great delight in picking out an uncommon word in an *Australian Geographic* story and buzzing various staff offices asking the occupants if they knew the meaning of the word. Frequently nobody did! To the frustration of the editorial staff sometimes, he demanded that the journal's text be aimed at high school English level, saying he wanted *Australian Geographic* to be read by 'the average Australian and not a select group of academics'. This made commercial sense too.

Don't spend on yourself until you can afford to

Often I've seen people who have started a business go out and lease new cars and office furniture, splurge on a prestige office or employ expensive people, all before the business has income to pay for them. When I first met Dick he was in a pokey office that had been the bedroom of an old apartment. The carpet was threadbare. He had placed fake timber panelling up against the bedroom wall but had never had the time to fix it there, so it was curling over at the top. One day when making a point to us he thumped his fist hard on his desk and, to our great glee, the pieces of panelling came down one after another, ending in a pile all over him.

But I soon learned that Dick had his priorities right—he paid himself a small salary and spent every cent on new stock to sell in the shop, on advertising and on producing his mail-order catalogue. You have to have a long-term view, the patience and the self-discipline to wait for your rewards. And you certainly will find it difficult to instil a sense of serious cost control in your fledgling business if your people see you treating yourself extravagantly.

Do business with people who risk their money

Be wary of a business investment where the sellers of the plan are not risking anything themselves. At Australian Geographic I was approached by two businessmen who wanted us to invest in a very successful overseas outdoor clothing chain for which they had secured the Australian franchise. I was interested, as we had a lot of respect for the brand and it was an area of retail we thought fitted well with our plans for expansion. The men were after an investment of $80 000, which wasn't a lot of money, but when I asked them how much they were putting in, their reply was none. They said they were not going to risk all they had and have mortgages placed on their homes. Well, if they didn't have enough confidence in their proposal to invest their money, we certainly didn't have enough confidence in them to invest ours. People who put their own money on the line will work harder at achieving success.

Talk to those who know

Nobody knows more about a business than the people who work in it. That seems obvious, but it puzzled me that we sold both the Dick Smith Electronics and Australian Geographic groups without the purchasers ever talking to our staff. If they had, they might have learned a lot more about the company's strengths, weaknesses and ways of doing business, and perhaps made some changes for a better fit.

It also intrigued me how the new owners took no opportunity to ask Dick or me in for an informal chat, or to invite Dick to speak at group staff conferences after we left. Neither of us felt personally slighted by this, but it didn't make *business* sense. If I were a young retail store manager attending one of the annual sales conferences and Dick Smith, the founder, came to address us about his early experiences and business philosophy, I would be on the edge of my seat! What motivation! For the new management not to have arranged it would be akin to having a major KFC sales conference down the road from Colonel Sanders's house and not inviting the colonel over to speak. I can only think that either it never occurred to them, or the management was somewhat insecure.

If you have access to someone who has done your job or run your company before, I suggest you ask their advice, have lunch with them occasionally or in some way involve them, especially if they were successful at what they did. But even if they failed, it would be good to learn where they went wrong so you won't make the same mistakes.

Don't be impressed by glamour or ego

I have seen magnificent shopping centres that won architectural awards but lost money. I have thumbed through glamorous catalogues that have won artistic awards but not

brought in a cent of profit. I have seen beautifully presented shop interiors that have won awards and the shop has
gone out of business. Don't necessarily be impressed by the
award winners, because behind the image there could well
be a loser.

Numbers of people you meet in business have very big
egos. (I have sometimes wondered whether their inflated
self-esteem has given them the confidence to get that far
and whether their ego will lead them into trouble.)
Companies, too, can become arrogant when they are successful. Their buying departments start treating their suppliers arrogantly, and the staff become disdainful of the
customers. I haven't met a lot of business leaders who
showed true humility and it was a refreshing change when
I occasionally did meet people like Paul Simons, the highly
successful former chairman of Woolworths; Peter Ritchie,
chairman of McDonald's in Australia; and film-maker
David Attenborough.

Have fewer meetings, and short ones too

Dick and I both hated having lengthy, unnecessary meetings, as neither of us had the patience. When Dick could-
n't avoid calling a meeting, you would hear his voice
booming out over our intercom system as he paged people
he wanted in his office—now!—for an ad-hoc meeting.
They would scramble to wrap up phone calls or just aban-
don everything and go. Sometimes, loud yelling and rant-
ing over the intercom would precede his call and we
would know a crisis had flared, so we would arrive in

some trepidation, but most times the room would be filled with laughter as Dick related a humorous incident that had just involved him or the company, or detailed an outlandish idea for a product or a publicity stunt and asked for feed-back.

Most of these meetings would be conducted as he field-ed telephone calls, with his secretary constantly interrupt-ing with announcements of appointments, or the names of people she had put on hold on one of his phones, for Dick did things 'in parallel'. These interruptions could be a wel-come escape route if somebody was being roasted over a deal gone sour or a company stuff-up, but most of the time I found Dick's ad-hoc meetings an entertaining relief from routine business. There was always a sense of urgency in the office. What needed discussing was quickly dealt with and everyone got on with running the business.

At other times, decisions would be quickly made and information passed on through our office intercoms, which were on almost every desk. Information might include the sort of brief announcement he made one morning when our intercoms suddenly crackled to life and Dick barked: 'My returns from commercial property investment this year are rotten. From now on, only plain biscuits for morning tea.' And he clicked off. The staff would have noted with amusement that Dick knew he never provided biscuits, either plain or fancy, for morning tea, but there really was a message there about watching costs.

Certainly this direct approach is easier to sustain in a medium-sized company like Dick's, but on the many occasions I had to sit through long meetings in large public companies, I would wonder what was being achieved other than a stroking of egos and a relaxing of backsides.

Have a sense of urgency

We encouraged fast-tracking of everything we did. We didn't spend a lot of time analysing a likely new product at Dick Smith Electronics: if the sample worked and the quality looked good we placed an order with the supplier right away. Some of our competitors would take weeks, even months, to get around to making a decision, by which time we had stocked the product and were selling it. Customers came into our shops because they knew we usually had the latest gadgets.

We made all sorts of decisions quickly without having lengthy meetings. With his boundless energy and enthusiasm, and his ability to work on many projects at once, Dick was great at encouraging a dynamic atmosphere. It really gave us an edge over our sleepy competitors.

When Dick was asked to speak publicly he gave a talk he called, 'Business by the Seat of Your Pants', which stressed the importance of speed and urgency in business. One thing that really frustrated him was how slowly drivers took off from traffic lights on their way to work. At that time there weren't as many automatic transmissions on cars as now, and he had noticed that in the United States and Japan the traffic got away more quickly—he felt there was a noticeable urgency about getting to work in those countries. He had a certificate made up that he handed out at

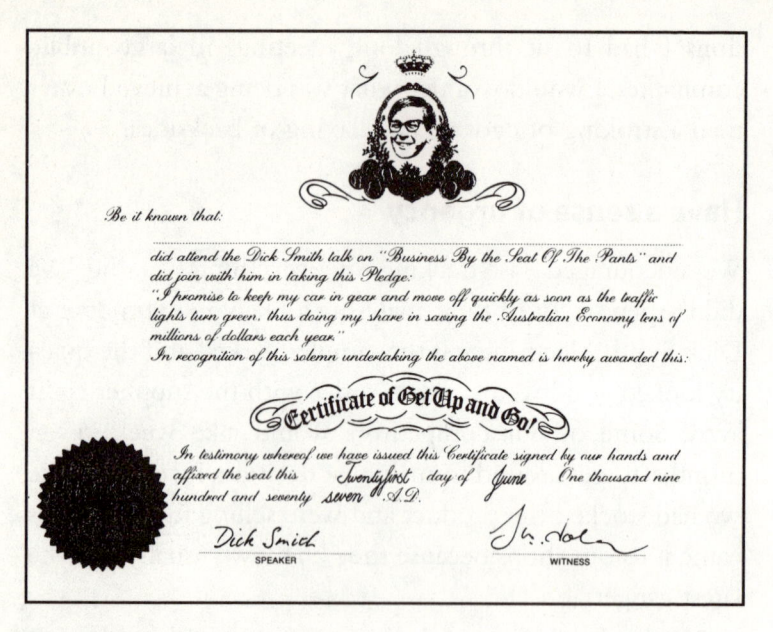

The Get Up and Go! certificate.

the end of his talk. It was the 'Certificate of Get Up and Go!', which pledged: 'I promise to keep my car in gear and move off quickly as soon as the traffic lights turn green, thus doing my share in saving the Australian economy tens of millions of dollars each year.'

Be democratic

At Australian Geographic I saw the need to open a store to extend our publishing activities. We were then selling by mail-order and the catalogue we had put together with a growing array of products, and which we mailed out with our journal, was booming. I was getting bored, and I could see the huge sales potential of a mailing list of over 200 000 names of *Australian Geographic* subscribers and other people who had bought gift subscriptions. For a year I pestered Dick to open an Australian Geographic shop—to no avail. Every time I raised the subject he would remind me, 'Ike, that's the reason I *sold* Dick Smith Electronics', but I did convince him to have a democratic vote of all our staff, and drafted the following memo:

To all Australian Geographic Staff

From Ike Bain

I would like to ask all staff whether they would like the company to be expanded further, or not. You are aware that Dick wishes the subscription level to be maintained at 200 000 and the company's retail activities to be limited to mail-order only. Some of us would like him to reconsider this decision. The nature of expansion anticipated could be:

Lifting the cap on subscriptions

A chain of Australian Geographic stores

A larger mail-order catalogue

More books published

Documentary films

More exclusive products developed

Of course, we must consider the possible negative effects of expansion. Some of these could include more people in the organisation, making the company less personal; the possibility of the company being more susceptible to downturns in the economy; more work pressures; more financial investment for Dick.

On the positive side, expansion can bring more opportunities for those seeking a career path, associated with greater responsibilities and financial rewards. If a company is involving itself in new projects, quite often a person can learn and experience different job/career directions without having to seek them elsewhere.

More sales could bring more money for the Australian Geographic Society and journal projects. More subscribers could mean that more people may learn about and appreciate the environment.

Or should we take a lead and see if a company can stop growing and still remain viable? Our philosophy is for less of a growth-orientated society; that the world cannot expect to keep growing and consuming at its present rate. Should we be one of the first companies that sets the example and says enough is enough, that we're happy to have 30 employees and only 200 000 subscribers?

Of course, we too may have to sacrifice some of our materialistic desires or personal needs, as presently our overheads are rising and, combined with inflation, the gap between our costs and what we sell our product for is diminishing. That could mean less money available to be paid out to employees. Could AG go out of business because it stood still and we stay the same size, become more efficient and maintain our present lifestyles?

Dick has always run a democratic company and would like to know what you all think. Some of the staff want the company to grow; some don't. What do *you* think? Please consider the points above and vote on what you wish to happen.

The votes came in. There were only two 'No' votes: they were from Dick and Pip Smith. We opened our first Australian Geographic shop a few months later.

Beware of growth for growth's sake

In our businesses we didn't just grow for the sake of growing. We pushed the companies quite hard to grow and I was always disappointed if we didn't have double digit growth in a year, yet we were cautious not to push too far. If something worked we would go further; if it didn't we knew we would not lose a fortune and had learned something.

When we opened that first Australian Geographic shop, I negotiated a lease for twelve months in a poor location up a flight of stairs on the first floor of an office building in York Street, Sydney, where the rent was dirt-cheap. We then spent a modest amount fitting out the shop, using second-hand building materials. From the day we opened the shop was packed, and that first year we turned over $1.5 million. In hindsight, the shop was successful because we had a new retail concept, loyal journal subscribers and unique products marketed well, with good service, so people sought us out in our poorly located shop.

We then thought we might be able to make the concept work in a shopping centre, so I went to Westfield and said I would like to experiment with a shop for twelve months at their large Chatswood centre. They were aghast. The shortest lease they signed was for five years. I asked them would they mind if I talked to Lend Lease or AMP, who also had centres. In the end, they agreed to the trial, but we remained cautious and took only a small shop of 60 square metres.

That year the shop was so packed at Christmas that we thought of putting on crowd-control staff to limit the time a customer would be allowed to shop in the store! We did end up hiring a security guard, just in case things got out of control. There was a long queue of people at the door wanting to get in, and others were three deep at the window, looking in to see what the fuss was about. Westfield immediately said we needed a bigger shop. I said no. I preferred to have a small, successful shop than a big, empty one.

After the success of those two Australian Geographic shops, we were inundated with requests for shops from shopping centres all over the country. It would have been easy to get caught up in the euphoria—we were on a winner—but we knew that nothing booms forever. We'd seen other chains on a roll, opening many stores quickly without worrying about site selection or taking time to negotiate the best deals: after a while they would go broke. We felt unforeseen circumstances might one day force a downturn in sales and we would be left paying big rents. So I told prospective landlords we would rank the centres in order of the rent deals offered us and then open only where we got the best deal and where we wanted to open next. All this was done with caution, but it was done with speed once a decision had been made.

Do what your company is best at

Focus on your core business and what you are best at. Too often I've seen a company go on an acquisition binge, buying up a lot of non-related businesses at high prices, some of which go bad and pull down what were once its main interests. The profits drop, management slashes over-heads, the cash flow declines, product development and marketing plans are abandoned, and morale dips when key employees jump ship because they see what is happening. At this stage the board brings in a new CEO, the bad acquisitions are sold and the company returns to its core business—with a heavy burden of debt.

When taking on a new post

If you have just been appointed to a senior position, don't be in a rush to change anything. Tell your people you think you might like to do this or that, but that you want to be sure the change is helpful. Ask for lots of advice. When you have all your information and you feel confident about making your moves, still discuss them with your people just in case you overlooked something. Try also to pace the changes. We found if you have too many changes taking place you can alienate your staff. The less hurried approach will also give you the opportunity to sniff the staff politics, and know who is pushing what agenda. Quite often we found that the people who talked the best and even seemed to be the best, were not the best—they were just better at acting.

On being a CEO

One of the most challenging roles of a CEO is to keep the company on course. Staff will want to have an input and some ideas will be very good and some disastrous. It's a balancing act to listen, have the patience to explain why some things can't be done and some can, and be firm in holding tight to your vision when you believe your company's standards, and its success, are threatened.

Surround yourself with the best people

It sounds obvious to suggest you should always surround yourself with the best people. Yet Dick often mentioned this as an important key to his success. You can't be good at everything and, in my experience, the most effective managers had the confidence to admit it. I got to think of the team that I worked with as a collective group of skills. Each had skills that I didn't have and my job was team coach. If the team worked well, the bottom line was healthy and we *all* looked good.

When necessary, be autocratic

There are times when an autocratic style of management is necessary. After we opened our Brisbane store we began to get bogus cheques across the counter, but the local manager declined to follow procedure and ask customers for identification, such as a driver's licence, or home and work telephone numbers. He was adamant that Brisbane customers were not like Sydney customers, and they would see such a request as an invasion of their privacy. I told the manager he could continue to do it his way provided he took personal responsibility for bogus cheques and that we would deduct the amount of each bad cheque from his bonus (his bonuses were linked to the profitability of his store). The manager went along with this—but changed his mind after he was defrauded a number of times!

Another manager refused to display price tags on expensive merchandise in the showcase, his view being that when a person asked for the price it would give him the opportunity of doing a selling job on the item. This was crazy, because at busy times customers would walk out when they couldn't find anyone to give them the price, and money or time were wasted while sales staff looked the price up or, in desperation, simply guessed it. We gave the manager the ultimatum of doing it our way or working for somebody who would let him do it his way. He eventually left, believing our way was hopelessly wrong.

Then there was the manager who was convinced that her product range had to be different from the products in all our other stores. Customers in her city were different, she said. She wanted to buy in stock direct from local suppliers in her state. We refused to change a thing. She revised her attitude and her shop went on to make a fortune.

There was always the issue of staff uniforms. Either they were too big or too small, too long or too short, too hot to wear or too cold, inclined to get dirty, inclined to be left at home, and certainly always the wrong colour and the wrong fashion. There was *never* the perfect uniform and I was convinced there never would be one. Finally we bought a heap of aprons all the same size and colour and said, 'Wear those!'

As I have said elsewhere, managing your company democratically is definitely the best way to gain the strongest commitment from everyone, but there are times when the leader has to step in and make a firm decision.

Get rid of the elite trappings

One of the first things that struck me when Dick Smith Electronics was bought out by Woolworths and Australian Geographic by Fairfax was the working conditions of their CEOs. You have to be careful of the message you send out to the people in the company. You can't get serious about cost control if employees see the hierarchy enjoying an expensive office renovation, being chauffeur-driven to work, having their morning tea served to them from a cart laden with silverware and having a company butler prepare them a favourite meal for lunch. It's not good for communication, either, when there are locked-off office areas, or even an elite floor that you need a special pass to get into. How intimidating this must be to someone who wants to talk to management about a great idea to make the company money or a complaint that could have been solved before an industrial walkout was thought necessary.

In the mid-1990s I returned to Woolworths to see Paul Simons after he had changed the company culture of the mid-1980s. No longer did I go through a security check. I simply got on an elevator and went, not to a lavishly fitted out top floor, but to a very basically appointed lower floor. This time I wasn't met by a receptionist. There was just a sign with two arrows: one pointing to Buying, the other to Management. I rang a bell. Paul Simons appeared, asked me if I wanted a coffee and took me to an instant coffee bar with plastic cups where he made me a coffee himself. I was

impressed. I knew why Woolworths was now making so much more money for its shareholders. Here was a chief executive who practised what he preached.

In support of dissent

Encourage your people to have enough confidence to stand up to you in discussions about company issues. In many companies the employees are intimidated into not saying what they believe because it may be politically incorrect with management or owners. Dick and I never sacked anyone for disagreeing with us, for stating their strong opinions or saying what they believed. There was a constant stream of people through our offices challenging the way we did things and we both sometimes had heated discussions with people with different views, but we did not discourage this exchange. We said, 'Look, these are the strict company procedures and policies and you're to follow them, but if you have a better way of doing things and there's a general consensus that we should change them, then we will.' As a leader you have to be strong, but you want people to know that you will listen and that they can stand up to you when they believe in something.

Try not to make the same mistake twice

I have often admired Dick for the efforts he will go to to see he doesn't make the same mistake again. He was always quick to put in place very strict guidelines when a mistake happened. He told the story to new staff about why we were so tough about having everything in our shops price-marked. He had opened his car-radio business and hadn't made a sale so left for several hours to see if he could drum up business. While he was gone his only employee, John Webster, made a sale of a radio aerial, his first sale, and he couldn't wait to tell Dick the good news. Dick was ecstatic and asked John how much he had sold it for. John said he didn't know the retail price so had looked up the cost price, put $1.50 on that and sold the aerial for $4.50. Dick was horrified, 'But John, that was a special purchase and the selling price is actually $6'. John said not to worry, 'we made $1.50'. Dick said, 'No, John, we *lost* $1.50!' Dick immediately went up to the newsagent, bought stickers, handwrote all the selling prices on them and price-marked everything in the small sales office. Many years later I would find him quietly checking stickers while visiting some of our Australian Geographic stores.

Chapter 15
On managing stress

Life isn't stress free

Business does seem to be moving at a more frenetic pace. Communication is fast, people want answers and decisions quickly and there is a greater demand for better quality and better results. Change seems to be constant in many businesses because of new technology, mergers, takeovers, liquidations, competition and globalisation.

I don't think that you can live a stress-free life in business, and I think a little stress may even bring out the best in some people. Not all the many times I have felt stressed in business have been bad times; some I remember as the best of times. It's when stress becomes constant and unrelenting that it becomes harmful. While there are many good publications on stress management written by experts in this field and worth consulting, what follows here are observations from my own experience, and some stress-relieving tips that worked for me, or that I saw work for others.

Put stress into perspective

When someone came to me panicking about a crisis or impending disaster I would say, 'Okay, what is the worst thing that could happen here?' Usually, after we had discussed the situation we found the predicted measure of doom had been exaggerated. This is usually the picture you paint for yourself when under stress. Limit your concerns to the things you can change and not those you have no control over.

We had a very good shop supervisor who was always anxious about the quality of her work. She felt she was letting down the business because she couldn't visit every shop as often as she thought she should. The truth was that she was trying to do more than she could manage, and in that situation she was feeling overwhelmed. She finally accepted that she was doing the best job she could with the time and the resources that were available to her: she could not be expected to do more, and nor did we expect her to do more.

Say 'no' more often

If you are an achiever it's easy to say, 'Yes, I can do that', and take on more work. It gives you a sense of being needed and, if you like the work, you probably enjoy doing it anyway. But you may take on more work merely because you are afraid to say no. It becomes a problem when you take on so much that you aren't able to maintain quality and achieve deadlines, and so you begin to let others down. I know a builder who says no, and he has a twelve-month waiting list. Everything he does he does well, and because it's difficult to get him, everyone wants him even more! I know people who ruined promising careers because they took on more work than they were capable of doing well.

They lost their good reputation and some were even sacked for incompetence. So thank the person for offering you the extra job, say no and explain you would very much like to help them but are afraid you would disappoint them because of the attention you must give to your current commitments.

Manage your time

A lot of unnecessary stress is caused by poor time management. It took three months to produce an issue of the *Australian Geographic* journal, and I think 80 per cent of the work was done in the last 20 per cent of the time available. It's difficult at the beginning of a project to create the same sense of urgency as exists when a deadline is close at hand.

We once had a purchasing manager who would work weekends and be constantly in a state of panic over all the work he still had to do. I noticed that he often had a social chat in the office or would seem to spend a lot longer on the telephone to place an order with a supplier than was necessary. I had a talk with him about this. He defended his style, saying it was important to build rapport with his people. In the end he couldn't cope with the workload so we appointed a new manager. Both staff and suppliers were very disappointed at this fellow's departure.

The contrast between him and his replacement was amazing. The new manager never worked weekends, wasn't at all stressed, always had an organised office and even began new projects. What was also different was that his office socialising was minimal, and when an order was placed with a supplier it was done quickly. Meetings were also kept brief. I did wonder, though, how the staff and suppliers would react to the new man and whether the change would affect staff morale.

It was quite incredible: in a few weeks I was getting comments from both staff and suppliers about the manager's efficiency and organising ability and how he didn't 'waste so much of our time talking to us'. Staff morale rose sharply because of the manager's enthusiasm and energy, and because staff were less stressed too. It's not how much time you have to do a job, it's what you do with the time.

Allow for unscheduled events

A lot of the times we came unstuck in our business were when we didn't allow enough time for events we couldn't have predicted. This was more likely to happen when we were doing something for the first time. Nearly every project we did had something new thrown in that we had never experienced before but that had to be resolved. So you'll save yourself stress if you allow extra time to deal with the unforeseen. Knowing you have done that may itself reduce your stress when the unpredictable happens.

Have a good rapport with your boss

Your work relationship with owners, managers, supervisors and team leaders is a common cause of stress. You've got to have a good rapport with the person you report to, but don't depend on it being a stress-free relationship. In business there are some aggressive, uptight people who enjoy putting others down, and if their remarks keep you awake at night they've got the better of you, which is what they wanted! But if their behaviour is constantly unreasonable, demanding or bullying, confront them about how you feel, and point out that you can do a better job for them if they treat you with more respect.

If it's their incompetence that is causing you stress, your problem is harder to resolve. If they're so entrenched in the company that their incompetence is unlikely to be acknowledged, your options are to risk reporting it, put up with it or find another job. Judge your chances of success before deciding to lobby your superior—and have an escape route to another job in case of failure.

Keep busy—and delegate

Dick told me his key to handling stress was to keep busy, but I also observed another way he managed stress. He delegated work that was adding to his stress to someone else, and had them take responsibility for it. Not all of us are in a position to do this, but sharing the burden with someone else you work with can help.

Do something *now!*

For me, the best way to reduce stress was to write down what was causing the stress and to come up with an active plan to confront the cause and resolve it. I found that postponing action, or avoiding it, only made the stress more difficult to manage. My stress began to diminish as soon as I began to act. By all means talk to people you trust, for it may help to formulate your strategy—but do it now.

Avoid back-stabbing colleagues

It seems to me that one of the greatest causes of stress in the workplace is simply the act of dealing with other human beings. The art of forging and fostering good relationships is not one we get a lot of training in, and some of us are just not good at it. Office politics, back-stabbing, manipulation, infighting over promotion, favouritism, all add up to a disruptive, distracting and stressful working environment. I know companies that were ripped apart by people saving their own skins and furthering their own careers when they could have been building a profitable business. In some companies this behaviour is so ingrained in the culture that it will flourish despite a leadership change. If you're in a company where the management condones, even participates in, office brawling, get out of it as soon as you can. You want to work in a company where the focus is on bringing the best out of people and where you're not constantly stressed by having to look over your shoulder.

Be prepared

Nearly all the things we are stressed and worried about never happen. One of the best stress relievers is to prepare for the worst by having plans in place for it. We tried to plan escape routes for such things as the loss of journal artwork on its way to the printer, for a transport strike at Christmas leaving our shops without inventory, for the resignation of a key person at a crucial time, and even for a massive downturn in business. Having a plan and possible escape routes will give you confidence to handle most situations, if, in fact, they do happen. Dick was particular in arranging back-ups and escape routes for his many flying adventures.

Don't fall for the trappings of success

I noticed that some people we gave bonuses or good salary increases to would use the money to fund further borrowings or would otherwise spend up to their new income. I know executives on huge incomes who are very stressed funding their lifestyle. They work weekends and haven't much time for their family because they are paying off a home larger than they need, a weekender they rarely have time to visit or a boat they seldom use. And because they have experienced the trappings of success, they find it difficult to downsize and reduce their stress.

My personal tips on avoiding too much stress

- A brisk walk or a jog early morning or at night gave me time for reflection, time to put things in perspective.
- I kept photographs in my desk drawer of three of my best loved places. They gave me peace at very busy times.
- In the car I had audio tapes of inspiring speakers and an enjoyable and uplifting selection of music.
- On plane trips I asked for a window seat. For some reason looking down at the earth also put things into perspective, and it was also a great time for planning.

- I found it helpful to think about what was going *right* in our business, and not necessarily dwell on what was wrong.
- We had a laugh, a joke and some fun whenever we could. The last thing you need when you're stressed is to be with someone who is negative, whingeing, angry or uptight.
- I always reminded myself that nobody handles stress well when they're tired. It's surprising how your outlook changes after a good night's sleep.
- I found good nutrition important. If you're working late in the office, watch the amount of fast food you consume, as well as the amount of caffeine, alcohol or nicotine.

Keep your life in balance

It isn't possible to keep your life in balance all the time. Often I found that life has to be out of balance to get to the next stage or to reach a goal. You may be facing an important deadline at work or the opening of a new business, dealing with family illness or a baby who keeps you up all night, or your own health problems. They are part of life but if they keep you off balance for long periods they can take a toll.

I know a few executives who live only for their work and their family life is a mess. They don't know their children, they've been through a divorce or two and they've neglected their health for years. Take their work away and they haven't much of a life. I was certainly a candidate for all this if I hadn't, in my late twenties, met my wife, Louise—a wonderful, supportive person who introduced me to a life outside work.

You can, of course, go too far the other way and give your family and social life so much attention that you neglect your work. I noticed the happiest people in business seemed to be the ones who lived for work when at work, but also invested time with family and friends, and took their regular holidays. They were better adjusted, more energised, less stressed and produced better work.

Chapter 16
On personal success

Do what you have the talent for

Don't waste your time trying to do something you will never be good at or to be someone you can never be. Be yourself and fulfil your own ambitions, but believe in what you do and your work will be a lot more satisfying. If you can't be loyal to the person you work for, work for somebody you can be loyal to.

If you make a mistake ...

I found it quite rare to work with somebody who would quickly admit, 'Yes, I stuffed up on that one!' without me having to ask a lot of probing questions first. It was refreshing to hear someone take responsibility when things went wrong, instead of attempting to shift the blame.

It always diffused our anger or frustration when someone would voluntarily inform us of their mistake. Dick used to say that when it comes to fixing mistakes, two heads are better than one. He's right. If you make a mistake, tell someone you think is the best person to help you fix it—and then promptly tell your immediate boss. If you delay reporting the mistake, it can look like a cover-up.

Don't hide it from your colleagues when it's fixed either: everyone can learn from mistakes. And if you are a senior executive who stuffs up, don't hide behind a team of lawyers!

Don't worry about your job title

Early in my career I installed a new manager in one of our suburban electronics stores. We were still setting up the store and I was helping the staff get it ready for our opening. Amid the chaos and the pressure to meet our deadline I noticed the manager was preoccupied with placing his name and title on his office door. I thought that fellow wasn't going to last long, and he didn't.

Off with the old, on with the old

A lot of people seek new jobs believing that the frustrations they have been experiencing in their old one will disappear. All that happens is that they swap the old frustrations for new ones. There is no job or project that doesn't have its frustrations and difficulties, and I've very rarely met anyone who doesn't think someone else they know has a more interesting job. I know from talking to many people in many careers that all jobs have their share of boring routine. Probably 70 per cent of what we did in our businesses was routine; it was the other 30 per cent that made it worthwhile.

Many people I have worked with over the years could have done far better in the company if they had been just a little more patient. Many left just at a time when things were beginning to work out for them, and you would find them going from job to job, blaming each company for not recognising their true potential.

And don't make a major decision, such as changing your job, when you are feeling down or fed-up. Being on a low can cloud your reasoning, and you may feel differently when you are not stressed or over-tired.

Be modest with predictions of future success

If you are modest with your predictions of future success you'll almost look like a winner if you fail! I thought Dick was a master at this. He would often lower everyone's expectations by saying things like, 'We'll probably go broke' or 'I'll bring out eight issues of *Australian Geographic* or lose $2 million—whichever comes first'. I'm sure he knew he stood a good chance of success. He called it 'the negative sell', and it works.

Avoid confrontation when your judgment is distorted

Early in my career I used to confront people about mistakes or breaches with guns blazing. I usually said things I regretted, which resulted in resentment from the employee or supplier concerned. I realised I had to find a more mature way of dealing with this, so I tried to delay a confrontation or refrain from reaching for the telephone until I was sane again. I would like to claim I fully mastered this technique, but I haven't entirely.

I'm more successful when it comes to putting my missiles on paper. After writing a critical memo or letter with more heat than is warranted, I often put it aside for a day. If it then reads like highly charged gibberish I throw it in the wastepaper basket; otherwise I rework and modify it.

Remember, your health is your most important asset

Several years ago I had a tumour removed from my spinal cord. I had been told for years that I just had a bad back and that I had to get used to living with pain. I was surviving on painkillers and during a period in hospital began to appreciate how drug addicts must feel as I waited anxiously for the rush of euphoric pain relief from the pethidine injections. In frustration I discharged myself, and it was only when I displayed symptoms of paralysis that I was properly diagnosed. I was told I would have a fifty-fifty chance of walking again after the operation to remove the tumour. I was lucky. The operation was successful and that whole drama was a good wake-up call.

Let me tell you that when you are seriously ill you don't think of your next business deal. Nothing matters except your family and your health. Possessions, job status, career—you would give these away to get your health back. It is so easy to get so caught up in the business chase that you forget to maintain your major asset: you. Take the time to look after yourself.

Get the facts before you criticise

It seems an obvious lesson, but often someone would come into my office complaining about a work colleague or a decision that had been made by someone, only to back down completely when I got the other party to explain the reasons for their decision. You never appreciate how difficult, demanding or detailed a job is until you have done it yourself.

Work at what you enjoy

I've noticed that people who enjoy their work the most work in an area that they are most interested in. It seems to give that extra drive and passion for what you do. Dick and I were at our best when our interests were matched with our work. We loved electronics, nature and the outdoors and that's why I think we had so much fun and enjoyment working at Dick Smith Electronics and Australian Geographic.

When Dick started *Australian Geographic* it seemed a natural fit. He grew up with a fascination for wildlife, a love of adventure, travel and exploration. Founding a journal that followed his interests gave him immense enthusiasm and the energy required in the embryo stage of the company. Aviation was another fascination for him and it took him to Civil Aviation Safety Authority where he ended up the chairman. Dick told me for years that he wanted to manufacture something in Australia, and starting Dick Smith Foods gave him the thrills that Dick Smith Electronics and Australian Geographic did. So try and work at something you have an interest in. If you can't do it right now, have that as a goal.

Work hard

A common feature I've noticed with all the successful people I've worked with is that they loved to work hard. A common feature with those I saw fail is that they didn't.

I noticed that the people who got ahead were not too proud to tackle any task that was available and needed doing. They completed the task enthusiastically and were willing to take on challenges. The biggest mistake you can make is to think you work for someone else. You work for yourself.

Success can lead to overconfidence

Be cautious when you are making decisions during buoyant economic times or when on a personal winning streak. It is easy to get caught up in the enthusiasm of the moment and to later regret your choices. We saw small chains start out well and then collapse because of a downturn in business when their fixed costs and borrowings overtook them. Overconfidence, and perhaps greed, led management to go beyond their limits. We were careful not to open one more shop than we could afford.

You're only as good as your last deal

Don't expect that a good negotiation, good work, long hours or the sacrifices you made to get the right result will be remembered for very long in the business world. There are always new targets. Achievements you made will be forgotten, and the people who might have supported you will have moved on. You will report to new managers and CEOs, or to others who will not be aware of your particular successes or really care, although not necessarily because they are insensitive.

Many good managers and leaders that I've met had very high standards and expectations and were never quick to dole out praise and reward. (The exceptional leaders do because they know it enhances performance, but they *are* exceptional.) You might be elevated, and briefly held in high esteem, if you have appreciably added to the bottom line—and then dispensed with when your contribution is considered to have diminished. But don't be disappointed if you don't always get the reaction you think you deserve. This is the business world. Adapt to it, or find a new career.

Think of the big picture

It always pays to think beyond the box you or the company has put you in. Many of our employees would express frustration that what they were doing was inconsequential to the success of the business. The truth was that what they were doing was important to the company's success: they just didn't *know* how it impacted on it. Sometimes this was due to poor supervision or communication by management—it suits some managers to keep employees in the dark. Don't let this deter you from finding out as much as you can about your job and how it impacts on the business. Research the rest of the company. Get a balance sheet, find out where the company makes its profit, who the senior management are and their history (there could be personal lessons for you there). The more you know about your company, the more valuable you will be, and the knowledge you have will give you a greater sense of purpose in doing what you do—and it will help you extend your horizons. Many people never seem to realise that their own success is usually in direct proportion to the success of their company. If you work hard to make the company prosper, you will likewise benefit.

If you want more money

The way to get more money is to increase your value to the company. Often people would come to me simply demanding a pay rise or a promotion in the belief that this was the way to get ahead. I would say that if they increased their value to the organisation, and it became very obvious they were contributing, they would become so valuable we would have to reward them more. You don't need to shout about what you have done, but you can quietly market your achievements. If your company truly doesn't recognise your value, some other company will.

Do the job you are asked to do

I had a direct marketing agency do work for us on occasions, but we didn't continue with them. We would have a briefing session where I would clearly outline what we wanted, and reinforce it by sending notes to the agency. They would return a couple of weeks later with all their creative work laid out for our final approval, and clearly they had put lots of effort into it. The problem was they had used nothing of what we discussed. They had gone down a completely different track!

Their response to our expressed dissatisfaction was they thought their ideas were better. They might have been, if they had run them past us first, when we might have saved them a lot of time and money. As it was, we could not use their creative input. They didn't know our business as well as we did and were unaware of all the commercial implications of their ideas. I found it amazing the number of people who don't do what they are directed to do when you are paying them to do it. The fastest way to success—or promotion—is to do exactly what your boss wants you to do, and with a sense of urgency. If you want to do it differently, get approval first.

Applying for a job? Read this

You won't believe the number of people we interviewed who had no idea about the business they were wanting to spend years of their life with. *Australian Geographic* editor Howard Whelan and I were interviewing a writer for our editorial department. The interview was going well for the applicant when a point arose about a journal article that neither Howard nor I could recall. 'Are you sure?' we asked. The applicant reached into his bag and triumphantly pulled out the article. It was from *GEO*, our competitor. He lost the job then and there!

I was always impressed by any applicant who had gone to our Dick Smith or Australian Geographic stores and asked what kind of company we were to work for, and could rattle off our history and statistics. It showed me they were serious. Their research also enabled them to ask us intelligent questions and demonstrate they understood our aims and requirements, which helped their application. Some applicants had even worked out our weaknesses and made suggestions as to where they thought they could best help us.

But a word of warning: check the company balance sheet and its financial reputation. You wouldn't believe how many people leave a secure job to join a company that's going broke. (Like me, for instance, when I first joined Dick Smith Electronics!)

Have a personal philosophy

I think a personal philosophy of life is good to have, for it helps you through the challenges and decision-making. Try to establish what you want to achieve, what kind of business you want to have, what type of leader or employee you want to be. When you have decided on these personal issues, you will have a much better understanding of the direction you want to take, both failure and success will be better managed, and you will be a happier and better directed individual.

Write your own history

Think of everything that you do as adding to your own history book. Once your history is written, there is nothing you can do to change it. I have told our children to look at their life as a history book, and each year as a new chapter. There will be adventure, challenge, happiness, sadness, fortune, opportunities, love—all these ingredients will make up their history.

Dick's CASHED-up formula for success

I once wrote down what Dick called his personal 'success forces'. They were:

1. Surround yourself with capable people.
2. Ask for lots of advice.
3. Enthuse others to perform.
4. Work really hard.

But he did, in fact, develop a more detailed formula, which he called CASHED, and he continues to quote it to anybody who asks for his 'secrets of success'.

C = *Communicate*

Communication problems in a company can cost a fortune and we were always amazed how they were often accepted as a normal part of doing business. We disliked bad communication and used to go out of our way to investigate, with witch-hunt thoroughness, why a breakdown had occurred. Dick would never assume that what he had said had been understood and seemed to be surprised when it was. In the early days of Dick Smith Electronics he had asked an electrician to install a light in his office ceiling, explaining there was a hidden joist there that it could be mounted on. The electrician got his apprentice to install the light but omitted to tell him about the joist, and he put the light in the wrong place and made a mess of the ceiling. When Dick tackled the electrician, the fellow said the apprentice was an idiot and he was going to sack him. But who was at fault? It was the boss who didn't tell the apprentice about the joist. Dick often used this story to explain why you had to explain in detail the reason you wanted something done, not merely make a request.

A = Ask

Ask for advice all the time. We found it seemed to be only insecure people who didn't ask for advice. We saved a lot of time and money by asking people for their opinions. Dick once told me that he believed asking questions and asking for advice was the most important reason he had been successful.

S = Simple

Keep things simple, and use commonsense. The advice in this book demonstrates the way Dick always kept things simple and used his commonsense.

H = Honesty

Dick would say the way to be successful was to be absolutely honest. Also see E = Enthusiasm.

E = Enthusiasm

Enthusiasm was one of Dick's greatest weapons when business was bad or we were confronting some special challenge. Over the years I knew Dick had his personal concerns and worries over the business but they rarely surfaced in public. What employees saw was generally an upbeat, enthused, positive fellow who was confident about the future. People rally to leadership that offers hope and optimism.

About eighteen months after Dick started the car-radio business there was a downturn and for days there were no customers. He would go out trying to drum up work, to no avail, and wondered if he was going to go broke. Then a customer drove in with his big Mercedes. Dick jumped in, flicked the radio on but found it working well. So he asked how could he help? The customer said he would like the radio fixed. Dick said there was nothing wrong with it. The customer asked couldn't he just do a bit of checking and charge him for it? Dick said he couldn't do that, and asked what was going on. The customer looked a bit sheepish and finally admitted that his neighbour had been to Dick's and was so impressed with his enthusiasm, despite the fact that he had so little business, that he had suggested the customer 'go in and see this young fellow, and give him some work'! Dick had two or three employees working for him at the time and you can imagine the impact on them if the boss had been negative and depressed about the lack of business. (While this story illustrates E for Enthusiasm, it could just as easily illustrate H for Honesty.)

D = Discipline

Dick would say discipline was the self-discipline of 'bloody hard work' and to be successful you had to put in the hard work.

What is success?

Finally, how does Dick define success? For Dick, the ultimate success is being able to do what you want to do. You can be a teacher, a park ranger or in a job where your income isn't necessarily high, but if you are doing what you want to do, then that is success.

THE BUSINESS RHYME

Communicate well - be crystal clear,
Copy if you can the success of others.
Manage as simply as possible - never fear,
Give little credit and ask few favours,
Business can be fun and your freedom is dear.

Dick Smith

Dick turned this simple message into a business card and passed it out to visitors asking for business advice

Index

Picture Credits

Cover, Page 4, 64, 65, 138, 139: Pip Smith

Page 23: News Limited

Page 25: Mike Wells 1979/ACME Cards UK

Page 17, 18, 29, 98, 127, 165, 177: DSE & Dick Smith

Page 33, 34, 43, 45, 69, 109, 110, 145, 187: DSE

Page 44: *San Jose Mercury News*

Page 52, 86, 95, 98, 101, 124, 126, 130, 196, 229:
Dick Smith

Page 71: Reproduced with permission of the artist

Page 84: Courtesy of Dick and Pip Smith

Page 93: *Dallas Times*

Page 121,134: The Fairfax Photo Library

Page 131: *The Herald and Weekly Times*

Page 133: DSE, Mike Middleton

Page 141,157, 176, 205: Loui Silvestro

Page 167: Rae Emery